ESTATE PLANNING MADE EASY

→ Your Step-By-Step Guide To Protecting Your Family, Safeguarding Your Assets & Minimizing The Tax Bite

DAVID T. PHILLIPS
&
BILL S. WOLFKIEL

Dearborn
Financial Publishing, Inc.

Publisher: Kathleen A. Welton
Associate Editor: Karen A. Christensen
Editorial Assistant: Kristen G. Landreth
Senior Project Editor: Jack Kiburz
Interior Design: Lucy Jenkins
Cover Design: Salvatore Concialdi
Illustrations: Bill S. Wolfkiel

Library of Congress Cataloging-in-Publication Data

Phillips, David T.
    Estate planning made easy : your step-by-step guide to protecting
your family, safeguarding your assets and minimizing the tax bite /
David T. Phillips and Bill S. Wolfkiel
      p. cm.
    Includes index.
    ISBN 0-7931-0612-5
    1. Estate planning—United States—Popular works. I. Wolfkiel,
Bill S. II. Title.
KF750.Z9P55 1994
346.7305′2dc20R
[347.30652]   93-38442
                                                                CIP

Dedication

We dedicate *Estate Planning Made Easy* to the thousands of Americans who have had the foresight, perseverance, patience, respect and love for their families, heirs and business partners to go through the estate planning process and take a proactive approach to fighting the uncertainty and often devastating problems that death inevitably creates.

More importantly, we dedicate this book to the countless thousands who have procrastinated on this critical phase of life planning because it seemed too difficult and cumbersome. For them, estate planning has now been made easy.

Furthermore, we dedicate this book to our clients throughout the country. Because of them, we were able to report on the real-life case histories contained within these pages.

Acknowledgments

We would like to acknowledge the ongoing contributions of our staffs, BDC, Inc., David T. Phillips & Company and Estate Planning Specialists. They have assisted us in many endeavors throughout the years with great responsiveness and creativity. Thanks especially to Rob Davis and Richard Hess, Attorney at Law, for their assistance on the creative end.

Also our thanks to Mike Ballard, Steve Briggs, Ray Bland, Gerald Clay and Arny Siegel for their support throughout the years. And to Bill Donoghue, Mark Skousen, Pete Dickinson, Julia Noble, Tom Phillips, Adrian Day, Richard Band and Terry Savage for their past endorsement of this needed American dream.

And a most sincere thanks to the affiliate offices of Estate Planning Specialists throughout the country for their unyielding assistance and patience in helping to hone the estate planning process into an easy-to-understand and -execute reality.

Contents

Foreword

When I went car shopping recently I was amazed at the incredible variety of choices. The market is saturated with hundreds of makes and models, foreign and domestic. After spending days visiting dozens of dealers, checking prices and comparing options, I became so dizzy with information that I couldn't make up my mind. In the end, I decided to stay with my old Ford Mustang.

That was a mistake. My transmission went out on me, costing me time and money. I knew it was time to get a new car, but the complexity of the car market discouraged me from acting. Now I was paying the price.

You might feel the same way when it comes to planning your financial future. Never in the history of the world have our financial lives been so complex with so many choices. Our investment portfolio used to consist of a few well-selected stocks and bonds. Now it contains foreign stock funds, foreign bonds, gold and silver, real estate, limited partnerships and other exotic choices.

Even estate planning has become a legal nightmare. A simple will is no longer sufficient. Setting up wills, trusts and other legal entities costs time and money. You have to deal with attorneys and insurance agents. You also have to contend with filling out lots of forms. On top of that, the tax code can be incredibly complicated—now you have to consider the nuances of income, estate, inheritance and gift taxes on the federal and state levels.

Many books attempt to lead you through this financial maze. In the end, you might throw your hands up in disgust and postpone any estate planning decisions, just as I procrastinated buying a new car.

That would be a mistake, a far greater mistake than my failure to buy a new automobile. *Failure to protect your estate and plan for your family's future can be disastrous.* You don't want to say at the end of your life, "Boy, did I leave my family and estate in a mess!"

What kind of mess? If you leave no last will and testament, your state makes one up for you, one that your heirs and family members might not like. If you have no living trust, your estate will be dragged through the probate courts, publicized in the newspapers and gutted by attorneys. If you haven't set up any estate protection trusts, the IRS can confiscate as much as 65 percent of your assets within nine months of your demise. No wonder so many descendants curse their ancestors! That kind of anxiety you can do without.

Fortunately, Dave Phillips and Bill Wolfkiel provide a comprehensive solution to allay your fears. Estate planning can be made easy! Of all the many estate planning books I have reviewed, *Estate Planning Made Easy* is the clearest, most precise and the highest in practicality. Each chapter outlines a problem in easy-to-understand terms and then provides a simple solution. Here is a book that finally lives up to its title!

As editor of one of the largest investment newsletters in the country, I have encountered hundreds of estate planners, insurance agents and other financial advisers, but Dave remains my number one contact for insurance, estate planning and charitable giving. His company, David T. Phillips & Co., was the first nationwide insurance agency, and it has helped to solve the financial needs of thousands of individuals. Not many people in this world can match Dave's gift for clarity, integrity and creativity. When Dave teamed up with Bill to coauthor this book, they created a perfect writing match.

Follow the counsel Dave and Bill outline in this book and you won't go wrong. Ignore it, and you'll be turning over in your grave.

—Mark Skousen
Editor, *Forecasts & Strategies,*
author, *Scrooge Investing,* and
coauthor, *High Finance on a Low Budget*

Preface

Have you ever been in the calm, waiting for an anticipated storm to strike? A ferocious storm approaches, but all you can do is watch helplessly. You can't stop it or alter its course. You know it's coming—it's only a matter of time. The clouds start to billow; the skies darken. And then it hits with all the fury you expected. The wind rages, upsetting and even damaging everything that hasn't been secured. Torrential rainfall follows hail.

Finally the storm moves on to devour another susceptible area. What seemed like hours was, in reality, only minutes. You assess the damage. Much to your relief, your losses are much less than your neighbors. You're thankful that you listened to the advice of the forecasters and prepared for the worst. Isn't it amazing that those who throw caution to the wind always end up suffering the greatest?

Sam is a 64-year-old corporate executive. Janet, Sam's wife, is also 64 and is unemployed. She has been active in charitable organizations most of her adult life. Sam plans to retire next year. He has worked for his present employer for the past 20 years. Over the course of his working years, Sam has paid as much as 63 percent of his annual income to federal and state income tax. Currently Sam and Janet are in a 43 percent combined federal and state income tax bracket. For each dollar Sam makes, he is able to keep only 57 cents.

Through prudent savings and investments, Sam and Janet now have assets worth $3.5 million. These assets include the value of Sam's qualified retirement program, which is approximately $1.5 million.

If both Sam and Janet die today, their estate will be taxed $1,371,500 in death taxes (federal and state estate taxes) before any other person or heir receives a penny. The IRS will require Sam's estate to pay this liability in cash within nine months after Sam dies.

Sam and Janet are facing a storm. However, their losses can be measured, and with proper planning they can avoid the ravage of this tax storm.

John lives near Los Angeles. A 72-year-old widower, he lives off the income from his commercial real estate. Valued at $4.3 million dollars, John's real estate has depreciated heavily in the past five years. He feels fortunate to keep all his properties rented and still maintain an adequate income from the rentals.

John is limited to only one unified credit or a $600,000 exemption against estate taxation at his death. If John or his estate makes full use of his exemption, John's remaining federal estate tax liability is $1,807,600. He fears that his real estate will be hard to sell unless he sells it at a bargain price. John's estate has no liquid assets to pay the federal estate tax at his death. John expects to lose 50 percent of his estate to taxation and forced sale of his real estate.

In addition to the federal estate tax liability, John has dodged two minor lawsuits brought by tenants in the past three years. He is looking for ways to protect his assets from the potential frivolous litigation that seems prevalent among landlords.

Fortunately, with help, John devised an estate plan that enabled him to gift some of his property to a qualified charity. Not only did he cut his estate tax by 43 percent, he also received a tax deduction in the year that he made the gift and is able to carry this deduction forward for an additional five years. These deductions against his adjusted gross income now provide John a higher annual net income. John replaced the value of the gifted property with a wealth replacement trust that allowed him to pass the entire value of his estate to his granddaughter. John also created two family limited partnerships and was able to structure these partnerships to protect his assets from potential future lawsuits. Thus, John has planned for and avoided the storm.

As a nation, we are in the middle of an economic storm. These questions bear answering: How prepared are we? How well will we as individuals weather this storm?

Early in 1992 Representatives Gephardt and Waxman, along with their long-term care bill for the elderly, proposed a reduction in the estate tax exclusion from $600,000 to $200,000. While most of us consider that old news, and the bill was tabled, most feel confident that something has to give with regard to current estate tax regulations.

At his preinauguration economic summit, President-elect Clinton responded to the question about the proposed decrease in the estate tax exclusion stating, "I'm not for it. I think it's about where it ought to be. However," he went on to say, "taxing capital gains at death should be looked at."

In 1993 the Clinton administration introduced and was able to pass the Revenue Reconciliation Act of 1993. Prior to this law the top estate and gift tax rate for decedents dying after 1992 or for gifts made after 1992 was 50 percent. This rate applied to taxable transfers over $2.5 million (see Chapter 8 for additional explanation of this new tax change). Under the new 1993 law, the tax rate on transfers over $3 million will be 55 percent. For taxable transfers over $3 million the rate reverts to pre-1993 rates or 55 percent. The new law actually reinstates pre-1993 estate and gift tax rates.

Such taxes could force families to sell the farm! Let's assume that you invested $100,000 in McDonald's restaurant stock 15 years ago and today it is valued at $1 million. Since your basis is $100,000, you determine that selling the stock would create a federal capital gains tax of $252,000 (28 percent of the $900,000 gain), and as such you cannot sell because you don't want to suffer a 28 percent loss; it doesn't make economic sense. Subsequently, you decide to leave the stock to your son at your death. Based on current law, your son can inherit the stock and receive a step-up-in-basis to the date of your death value. If your son sells the stock the next day for $1 million, there will be no capital gains tax due.

If the step-up-in-basis is eliminated, the gain would be taxed back to the original $100,000 basis, and your son would owe $252,000 in capital gains taxes, not to mention state income tax as well, payable the next April when taxes are due. That's over a 30 percent loss that will never be restored. Plus, the asset would still be taxed in your estate for federal estate tax purposes.

This step-up-in-basis provision as well as many current estate planning options and strategies could be in serious jeopardy if the current administration or future administrations look for ways to raise revenue.

One recent article reported that those in favor of taxing capital gains at death say the tax system would be fairer and would fuel the economy by reducing incentives for investors who hang on to assets until death. As it stands now, the law is both bad economics and bad social policy, according to adviser Robert Shapiro of the Progressive Policy Institute, who has devised one plan for changing the system. He says that the present system allows very wealthy people to escape normal tax liability.

This is hardly the first time the government has thought about taxing gains at death. The Tax Reform Act of 1976 actually included a form of the tax, but that provision was postponed in 1978 and repealed in 1980 before ever taking effect.

The storm is on the horizon. How it will materialize and what shape it will take are still unclear. What legislation the current administration will propose and proceed to enact is unknown at this writing. What will happen under future administrations is also unknown. Will we helplessly throw our hands up and surrender without mustering a defense? This would be as illogical as saying that there is nothing one can do to prepare for a hurricane. Our government has spent billions of dollars in an effort to predict where and when the "big one" will hit in order to minimize losses of both lives and property. They expect us to be prepared. They warn us and give us explicit directions and instructions on how to avoid loss of life and damage to our property. All this guidance for a potential natural disaster.

When was the last time our government warned us of pending legislation that could reduce our financial fortress to rubble? Surprise! You don't hear much from them on this subject. As financial news editor, Debbie Price, of the *Fort Worth Star-Telegram* recently stated, "Where death and taxes and Congress are concerned, what taxpayers don't know can hurt them." So, "mum's" the word.

However, this much we can predict with the accuracy of the national weather bureau: The rules we have become accustomed to during the last decade concerning estate taxation are subject to change, and those Americans who are considered moderately affluent ($600,000 net worth) and upward, and who do nothing, may be faced with devastation; that is, their children's potential inheritance will shrink or be devoured.

*T*he best defense is a good offense. And the best offense is based on knowledge. ◆

How can one prepare for the unknown? The best defense is a good offense. And the best offense is based on knowledge. With knowledge, you can aggressively pursue and attain solutions. What does our government and the current administration have in mind? Can we take steps to avoid hands that reach deeper into our pockets?

Unfortunately, we don't have a crystal ball and most of us are not clairvoyant. However, we can use what we have. How many people understand and are utilizing a well-thought-out strategy? How many people seek competent advice? How many people actually have a formal **estate analysis** of their current estate to identify problems and achieve their objectives? How many actually construct a **formal written estate plan** or **format** to achieve stated *objectives* and then proceed with the *execution* of the plan?

♦ **WARNING**

By not having an estate plan, family and heirs are subject to

- state laws that decide who will inherit your assets,
- settlement delays that could take years to solve,
- forced sale of assets to pay taxes and settlement costs,
- administrators appointed by the court and
- guardians for children appointed by the court.

When estate planning turns to talk about taxes, most people think of income taxes. Yet for many people estate taxes (death taxes) may be the largest single tax expense they'll ever face. With estate tax rates as high as 55 percent, the value of your estate could spiral downward to 40 percent of its original value before it passes to heirs. To put it another way, without proper planning you could lose more than half of what you've spent a lifetime building. Proper planning can often reduce or eliminate this harsh reality.

Annually, countless Americans begin the process of planning their estates. Frustrated by a lack of options, information and myths, the majority fail to complete an effective plan. In *Estate Planning Made Easy* we outline a method that will systematically help the individual, couple, business owner and executive identify and answer the following estate planning dilemmas:

- To whom, what and when do I pass my assets?
- Do I need a will or trust? Are there more appropriate tools available?
- Who will care for my minor children?
- What part of my estate will be lost through taxation?
- Should I use my attorney, accountant or financial planner to design my plan?
- What will it cost to complete my plan?
- How can I best pass my business interest?

- Will I lose control of my assets?

- Are there ways that I can disinherit the IRS?

- How can I create liquidity to pay my estate taxes?

These are just a few of the questions that each of us faces as we try to sift through the maze of planning options. Is it any wonder that most of us put off what seems a monumental task?

In reality it doesn't have to be so cumbersome or so complex. Estate planning can be simplified and yet be extremely effective. Indeed, *estate planning can be made easy.*

*T*aking action to plan your estate still remains your decision. ♦

We sincerely believe *Estate Planning Made Easy* will help you prepare a blueprint for your estate plan. We will show you various alternatives for passing your estate intact. You will learn strategies for reducing taxes and administrative costs. However, taking action to plan your estate still remains your decision. Postponing planning can result in current strategies being altered or lost forever as our government moves to close potential doors to widen the tax revenue base.

Remember: *Procrastination can be dangerous to your wealth!*

—Bill S. Wolfkiel and David T. Phillips

How To Use This Book

In an effort to address the needs of a wide variety of readers, we have divided this book into two parts:

PART I:
THE ELEMENTS OF EFFECTIVE
ESTATE PLANNING

Addresses the fundamental elements of estate planning. From property ownership, probate and various estate and gift tax regulations, it provides a basic framework for estate planning.

PART II:
ADVANCED STRATEGIES FOR ESTATE PLANNING

Takes an in-depth look at various estate planning strategies. For those readers familiar with the basic elements of estate planning, Part II provides actual estate planning applications and sophisticated techniques to help them format and execute an effective estate plan or modify an existing plan.

PART I

The Elements of Effective Estate Planning

CHAPTER 1

Estate Planning

It's Your Money and More

Estate planning is often touted as money planning. Who gets what, how much, when and how is it distributed? The real issue, however, is people and the problems they face at your death. Spouses, children, grandchildren, dependents, business partners and others will suffer not only emotionally but also economically if you fail to plan. Taking care of people problems is the main objective in estate planning. *Estate planning is people planning.*

In our business we meet wealthy people daily. We've always had a difficult time understanding why a substantial number of these people refuse to address their estate planning. Many have substantial (six-figure) estate tax liabilities at death. Recently we found the answer to this mystery. A client we had been working with for several weeks was having difficulty deciding on some basic estate planning issues. Although his spouse was concerned about problems that might occur at his death, he seemed to have a lack of motivation to address these issues. This individual finally informed us that he didn't expect to die, at least anytime in the near future. However, he is missing the point of estate planning: Until each of us realizes the probability of our own mortality, estate planning lacks meaning and definition.

We spend a lifetime raising families, creating income, taking care of people and planning for the future, and in an instant it can end. We lose our opportunity for a plan of continuation if we fail to plan before death. Estate planning is really living planning. It involves money—lots of it. Generally planning

*U*ntil we realize the certainty of our own mortality, estate planning lacks meaning and definition. ♦

takes time, thought and guidance and can appear complicated and confusing, but it can be simplified.

We have witnessed through the years that almost all of us already have an agenda. Most people, with a little thought, know what they would like to accomplish. The difficulty is finding outlets for guidance to complete the process. Each of us deserves understanding and a comfort level that will facilitate the process and eliminate the mysteries.

If you were drafting a last will and testament, which of the following would you prefer?

Last Will and Testament #1

Being of sound mind and strong body, I hereby stipulate this to be my last will and testament. To the *Internal Revenue Service,* my lifelong partner, I hereby bequeath one-half or more of all my assets—both business and personal—which I have been able to accumulate throughout a lifetime of endeavor.

I further stipulate that this bequest be satisfied in cash and that only the most liquid and readily saleable of my assets be utilized in fulfilling this bequest.

Last Will and Testament #2

With the knowledge and confidence that I have otherwise provided for the Internal Revenue Service, I hereby bequeath my estate in its entirety to *my personal beneficiaries* in accordance with the provisions of my last will and testament.

Attaining Last Will and Testament #1 is automatic. You need to do nothing to carry it out. Just sit back and relax, and our system of state and federal government will handle everything for you.

Attaining Last Will and Testament #2, however, will require some effort on your part. Primarily, it will demand the coordination of your financial and legal advisers to formulate and execute a plan for the proper distribution of your assets when you are gone. If your gross estate is worth $600,000 or more (which is not a whole lot these days), one integral part will be to provide the necessary funds to cover your estate tax bill when the time comes.

By making provisions today for estate liquidity tomorrow, you gain peace of mind knowing which part of your estate will pass to heirs and which part will go to the IRS!

THE ECONOMIC RECOVERY TAX ACT OF 1981 (ERTA)

In 1981 President Ronald Reagan signed into law the **Economic Recovery Tax Act of 1981,** commonly called **ERTA.** ERTA afforded substantial relief to many Americans in such areas as income taxes, capital gains taxes and gift taxes. The most significant relief was in the area of *estate taxation,* the assessment you pay to transfer your estate to your heirs.

Prior to ERTA, the tax rate on an estate valued over $60,000 started at 32 percent and quickly escalated to 75 percent. We distinctly remember hearing the sad story about the severe loss of Nat King Cole's estate during that time. When Mr. Cole passed away, his estate was valued at over $3.5 million. Unfortunately, after estate taxes and settlement costs, his daughter Natalie received less than $1 million.

The real tragedy of pre-ERTA estate taxes, though, was felt by landowners, particularly farmers. Since farmers traditionally kept little cash on hand, the surviving spouse was often forced to liquidate a major portion of the farm to cover the enormous estate tax bill.

With the passage of ERTA, things have changed for the better. That new law (1) introduced the **unlimited marital deduction** (the ability to pass applicable assets to a surviving spouse with no tax), (2) increased the estate and gift tax exemption amount to $600,000 per person and (3) restructured the tax rates. Most importantly, it left all of us the opportunity to plan our estates with less taxation and more options.

*I*f there is one specific caveat that we can offer the general public in their quest to properly plan their estates, it is to *seek professional help.* ♦

AVOID DO-IT-YOURSELF PLANNING STRATEGIES

In the past 15 years we have handled estate planning for hundreds of people. Estate size has ranged from less than $1 million to multi-million-dollar estates. If there is one specific caveat that we can offer the general public in their quest to properly plan their estates, it is to *seek professional help.*

This book addresses highly technical areas such as the following:

- Federal estate tax
- Generation-skipping transfer tax
- Excess accumulation estate tax (on retirement plans)

- Various revocable and irrevocable trusts
- Charitable gifting techniques
- Asset protection strategies
- Leveraged dollar method for paying taxes

These issues are applicable to both small and large estates. However, they have to be designed and implemented correctly. These are not do-it-yourself planning strategies. Through the years, we have witnessed individuals with good intentions who try to accomplish estate planning without proper help and guidance. The results have and continue to be devastating. Please make sure that you seek proper guidance before you attempt to create a plan. If you are unsure where to seek help, Chapter 3, "Assembling the Team," focuses on this dilemma.

CHAPTER 2

Objectives

What Do You Want?

Developing specific objectives and goals is the first step to creating an effective estate plan. If you are uncertain what your objectives are or should be, simply starting the estate planning process will usually provide a road map for you to follow. The first fundamental issues to deal with are *to whom, what, when* and *how* to pass your estate.

TO WHOM WILL YOU PASS YOUR ESTATE?

The following are some of the people and organizations to consider when you are deciding for whom you want to make provisions:

- Surviving spouse
- Children
- Stepchildren
- Parents
- Grandchildren
- Siblings
- Nieces or nephews
- Close friends
- Alma mater
- Other charities

Dividing your estate among these people or entities takes careful thought and consideration. For example, your death will have a considerable impact on your surviving spouse, especially if minor children are involved.

WHAT ASSETS WILL YOU PASS?

Quite often, assets are positioned in ways that make passage to certain individuals extremely costly, and sometimes disastrous. A business interest passed to children uninvolved in the business versus to children involved in the business and competent to continue the business operations can spell disaster for the continuity of the business. However, passing the business interest only to those children involved in the business may cause a lopsided distribution among those involved and uninvolved individuals. If equality is an objective, this raises the question of estate equalization among the various beneficiaries.

WHEN SHOULD YOU PASS YOUR ASSETS?

Should certain assets be passed during your lifetime (now) or at death? By gifting assets now, you may avoid inclusion of those assets in your gross estate at death, thus lowering or eliminating estate taxation. However, if these assets are highly appreciated, passing them at death may give the beneficiary a step-up-in-basis to date of death value, thereby eliminating or significantly reducing capital gains taxes when sold by the beneficiaries.

When you are trying to decide when to pass assets, consider the following specific objectives:

- Are you willing to give up the ownership, control and benefits of these assets during your lifetime?

- Will you jeopardize your future income picture or that of a surviving spouse if assets are disposed of now or before death?

- Can you ensure that your assets will pass to your surviving spouse at your death?

- At the death of the surviving spouse, will your assets pass to surviving children?

- Will disposition during your lifetime eliminate probable probate costs and delays? Will disposition now avoid or minimize estate taxes?

- Will there be enough liquid assets to provide for the payment of taxation and costs for settling the estate?

*F*ederal estate taxation and probate costs are difficult to assess unless you employ competent help. ♦

Each of these questions should be answered during the estate planning process. Federal estate taxation and probate costs are difficult to assess unless you employ competent help. This assessment starts with an in-depth look at asset inventory. Exact valuation of assets—and in particular business assets—can be extremely complicated to value. Most people try to utilize book value or some other self-predetermined valuation formula. It is important to understand that the IRS method of valuing your business or business interest may be extremely different from your formula. This can spell disaster in cases where business interests are valued low and improper planning results.

The IRS valuation method usually utilizes the following factors:

- Book value
- Capitalization of earnings
- Capacity to pay dividends
- Type of business
- Economic outlook expectation
- History of prior stock sales
- Goodwill
- Sale history of comparable businesses

Valuation of assets is just one element the estate planner should consider in the assessment of a current estate. The following list presents seven other elements involved in estate assessment:

1. How property is held and consequently how it will pass
2. What assets are considered to be probate assets
3. Probate costs
4. Federal estate tax and state tax cost at death
5. Estate shrinkage at your death and the death of a spouse
6. Liquidity needs for the payment of taxes
7. Future problems as the estate grows or matures

WRITTEN ESTATE PLAN SUMMARY

The previous seven elements are fundamental to assessing your current gross estate and identifying possible problems. In addition, once this information is gathered, your planner can then assemble, assess, communicate and illustrate unknown problems and solutions, such as potential and existing tax liability. This is usually presented in a **formal written estate plan summary** or *estate analysis*.

HOW DO I ACCOMPLISH MY OBJECTIVES?

*T*he formal written estate plan summary becomes the basis of estate planning. ♦

The **formal written estate plan summary** becomes the basis of estate planning. It identifies problems (such as tax liability, probate, who gets what and when) and presents planning opportunities to solve these problems or makes adjustments to previous plans. To determine how to plan your estate, you need to be familiar with the problems and then begin to **format** a plan utilizing the various estate planning tools available.

The basis of constructing the estate plan summary is the accurate detailed information gathered by the estate planner. This is usually accomplished by completing a comprehensive asset inventory form, which lists all assets and property owned and included in the gross estate. This inventory should also include an accurate breakdown of ownership. Figure 2.1 is an example of a simplified form we designed for asset inventory and pertinent information.

IS YOUR CURRENT PLAN EFFECTIVE?

If you have a formal estate plan in place or you have formulated one on your own, review or update it from time to time. The following guidelines will help you measure how effective your estate plan is since you first created and implemented it:

- Has your estate appreciated since your last planning was implemented?

- Have your goals or objectives changed?

- Have there been any deaths of beneficiaries or divorces?

- If you have created a living trust, have you funded it?

- Have you received an inheritance?

- Have you relocated since your last analysis?

FIGURE 2.1 Asset Inventory Form

PERSONAL ESTATE PLANNING PROFILE
CONFIDENTIAL

IF YOU ARE SINGLE, WIDOWED OR DIVORCED, SIMPLY PROVIDE YOUR PERSONAL INFORMATION
AND DISREGARD ALL REFERENCES TO A SPOUSE.

CLIENT'S FULL NAME			CLIENT'S FULL NAME (Spouse)		
DATE OF BIRTH	CITIZENSHIP	OCCUPATION	DATE OF BIRTH	CITIZENSHIP	OCCUPATION

HOME ADDRESS	CITY, STATE, ZIP	HOME PHONE ( )
MAILING ADDRESS	CITY, STATE, ZIP	WORK PHONE ( )

ASSETS AND LIABILITIES

HOW IS TITLE HELD?   KEY :   H=Husband's separate

CP=Community property   RLT= Revocable Living Trust
JT=Joint tenancy   TC=Tenancy in common
W=Wife's separate   TE=Tenancy by entirety

DESCRIPTION OF ASSETS	FAIR MARKET VALUE	LIABILITY	NET VALUE	HOW IS TITLE HELD?
RESIDENCE				
OTHER REAL ESTATE				
STOCKS AND BONDS				
BUSINESS INTERESTS				
CASH IN BANKS (CD(s), MONEY MARKETS)				
NOTES RECEIVABLE				
PERSONAL EFFECTS (AUTOS, BOATS, ETC.)				
RETIREMENT PLAN (NOT IN SETTLEMENT)				
OTHER ASSETS				
OTHER DEBTS				
TOTALS:				

LIFE INSURANCE & ANNUITIES (Please list additional policies on separate paper.)

COMPANY	INSURED	OWNER	BENEFICIARY	FACE AMOUNT	CASH VALUE

INCOME
JOINT ANNUAL GROSS EARNED INCOME $ _____   JOINT ANNUAL GROSS INCOME FROM INVESTMENTS $ _____

CHILDREN (LIST ALL LIVING CHILDREN: C=CLIENT S=SPOUSE J=JOINT)

NAME	AGE	SEX M F	PARENT C S J	NAME	AGE	SEX M F	PARENT C S J
NAME	AGE	SEX M F	PARENT C S J	NAME	AGE	SEX M F	PARENT C S J

GRANDCHILDREN (INDICATE SAME AS FOR CHILDREN)

NAME	AGE	SEX M F	GRANDPARENT C S J	NOTES:
NAME	AGE	SEX M F	GRANDPARENT C S J	

- Have there been any children or grandchildren recently added to your family that should be considered?

- Do you have an insurance trust to remove your life insurance from your gross estate?

- Are you making use of your annual gift tax exclusion?

- Have you used your unified credit ($600,000)?

- If you have married, have you made provisions to utilize both your and your spouse's unified credit for a $1,200,000 deduction?

- Are you gifting highly appreciating assets to effect an estate freeze?

- Are you familiar with the advantages of charitable remainder trusts?

- Is there adequate liquidity to pay estate taxation and death costs?

If you have not recently addressed any of these questions, we recommend a complete review.

The real value of the estate planning summary is to identify specific problems that each one of us may be unaware of in our own estates. Quite often clients will have established goals in mind, such as the who, what, when and how to pass their estate. By producing a formal estate plan summary, problems can be identified and defined and then coordinated with the balance of the estate planning objectives. The type of problems that are ultimately identified by the summary process varies greatly. The most common are improper property ownership, identifying probate assets, assessing estate tax liability and providing an accurate picture of any current estate planning in place.

CHAPTER 3

Assembling the Team
Finding a Quarterback

Constructing an estate plan takes professional help. Deciding who will help you accomplish your estate planning goals is probably the most crucial step in achieving your overall objectives. This decision is complicated by the enormous number of people who refer to themselves as **estate planners.** Today estate planners come in all sizes and shapes. The choices are wide open: insurance agents, financial planners, investment firms, bank trust departments, attorneys and those who devote 100 percent of their time to the practice of estate planning.

How do you decide whose advice and guidance to seek? Perhaps the best way for you to make the selection is to have a set game plan from the start. But to have a game plan, you must first understand the game!

Almost everyone has watched an occasional football game on television. Have you ever watched a game in which an injury sidelines the starting quarterback? How well does the team perform? Most often teams are decimated when the star player or the person who directs the team is out. In fact, quarterbacks who are lost for long periods due to severe injury cause losing seasons for most teams.

Winning the game of estate planning requires similar coordination and direction by a team leader. A person with the experience and resources to effectively direct and execute a plan can mean the difference between success and failure. This becomes quite clear when you begin to explore the various aspects involved in estate planning.

A person with the experience and resources to effectively direct and execute a plan can mean the difference between success and failure. ♦

FIGURE 3.1 Three Basic Elements of an Effective Estate Plan

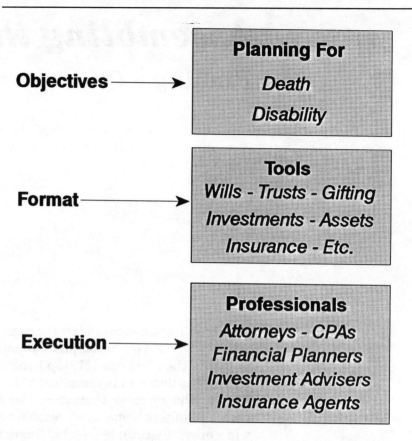

ATTAINING AN EFFECTIVE PLAN

There are three elements basic to attaining an effective plan: (1) **objectives**, (2) **format** and (3) **execution**. In Figure 3.1 these elements are categorized to illustrate each stage.

Objectives

Objectives in estate planning are not limited solely to death planning, testamentary planning and disability planning but lifetime planning as well.

Format

Format planning consists of the various tools to facilitate objectives. In simple estate planning there may be only one tool, a will. This tool facilitates the distribution of assets at death and usually indicates a nontaxable estate. However, the typical estate plan today contains many sophisticated tools designed to achieve any number of planning objectives.

Execution

Execution, once a plan is formatted, generally requires the use of an attorney to facilitate plan documents such as wills and trusts. The plan usually is coordinated with additional professionals such as financial planners, investment advisers and insurance agents. Valuing assets, retitling assets, measuring life insurance proceeds for inclusion in the gross estate, assessing tax liability and many other elements are all integral parts of total estate planning.

ESTATE PLANNERS AND QUARTERBACKS

In the past five years we have seen the advent of the **estate planner.** These individuals, and their staffs, concentrate their efforts on and specialize only in estate planning. Their backgrounds are varied. Many hold business degrees, some are attorneys or Juris Doctors and others have extensive backgrounds in financial services and now specialize in the area of estate planning. These individuals and firms have specialized in estate planning because of two factors: (1) the degree of sophistication in planning techniques required to be effective and (2) the need for systematic efforts across the United States to bring about entities that specialize in specific areas of estate planning. Examples of such specialized areas are business succession, estate freeze techniques, wealth transfer, charitable gifting and generation-skipping transfers.

Such hybrid planners are often referred to as **quarterbacks.** They usually facilitate objectives, format and execution. These essential elements of planning are often integrated and achieved under one roof because the professionals are structured for and integrate all the various aspects of planning.

The quarterback method of planning does not exclude other established professionals the client may have. The quarterback simply coordinates the entire process with these other individuals and fills any voids where necessary. His or her most important function is to develop a written plan and familiarize all those involved in the process with the objectives, format and execution of the plan.

Figure 3.2 illustrates how this method can be simplified. In the *client maze,* the client is faced with the multifaceted job of coordinating all the various aspects of the plan. In the *client simplification box,* the client allows the quarterback to facili-

FIGURE 3.2 The Quarterback Method versus the Client Maze

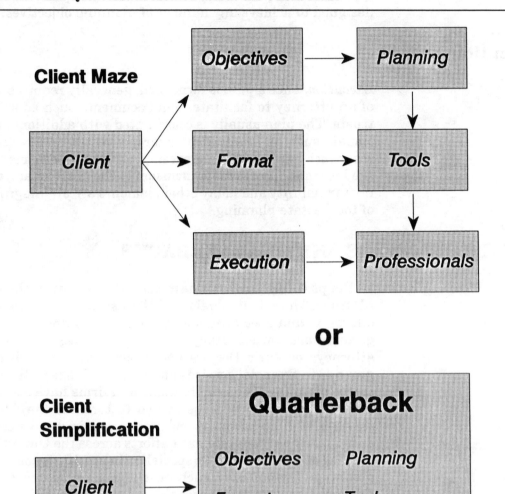

tate all the various components of the plan. This approach usually eliminates the confusion most people feel when planning their estates.

Finding the right planner should consist of finding a planner who can coordinate all the various aspects of your plan. This includes the coordination of objectives, format and execution under one roof with all of your advisers. Coordination of the various tools that will be used and combining all the various professionals usually provide a clear, concise and effective plan.

CHAPTER 4

Ownership and Title
The Built-In Estate Plan

*I*f assets are not titled properly, your estate plan may prove to be ineffective. ♦

In one of our recent client meetings, our client (let's call her Mary) divulged that she had arranged to give her house, which she currently shares with her husband, to her daughter upon death. Mary had recently remarried after being a widow for several years. The house was titled in joint tenancy with right of survivorship with her current husband. When we asked her how she intended to facilitate the transfer of this property, she said that she had made a provision in her will. Unfortunately, as we pointed out, based on how the house was titled with her new husband, it would pass directly to her husband upon her death by **operation of law.** Her daughter would not be entitled to inherit the house. Mary had no idea that her will had no effect on passing the house to her daughter.

This situation provides a good example of why accurate information gathering is vital. In this case it revealed a potential problem with Mary's current estate plan based on her actual goals and objectives.

To explain how property passes, we must review how certain property is owned and the potential problems various forms of ownership present in passing property at death. But first, there are two basic forms of ownership: (1) property that is owned by one person (**outright ownership**) and (2) property that is held in conjunction with others (**joint ownership**).

OUTRIGHT OWNERSHIP

Property that is owned completely by one person or individually is the simplest form of ownership. This type of ownership is referred to as outright ownership or **fee simple** ownership. With this type of ownership, an individual is free to accomplish all the various provisions ownership provides without the consent or constraints of other people. The owner has the freedom to sell, exchange or manage the property in any way that corresponds with his or her desire. The owner can collect any income that is applicable to the property, profits from any gain and suffers from any loss and also assumes all liability that goes along with property ownership. Examples of liability include maintenance, repair, taxes and debts that may be secured by the property.

JOINT OWNERSHIP

Unlike outright ownership, which deals with ownership by one individual, joint ownership has several different forms and can be more complex. The types of joint ownership consist of the following:

1. Joint tenancy
2. Tenancy by the entirety
3. Tenancy in common
4. Community owned property

Joint Tenancy with Right of Survivorship (JTWRS)

This type of ownership provides for any number of owners. All owners hold an equal undivided share of the property. If the property is disposed of, it must remain undivided. A tenant is free to sell his or her share of the joint tenancy. The new owner will own his or her interest with the other tenants and not as a separate share.

You cannot readily sell your interest as a separate share or as a separate part. Shares can be separated only under the direction of a court, more commonly referred to as remedy of *partition*.

Example

Mary Williams and Sam Perkins own stock as joint tenants. The value of the stock is $500,000. As joint tenants, each owns an equal share of the stock or 50 percent. If Mary wants to sell her interest, she cannot divide or separate her interest from Sam's interest. A new owner will continue as a joint tenant with right of survivorship with Sam Perkins. If one of the two tenants dies, the survivor will succeed to full ownership.

Another interesting feature of joint tenancy deals with how the property passes at the death of the tenants. At the death of a tenant or co-owner, the surviving co-owners acquire the decedent's entire interest in the property by law. If you are a surviving tenant, the total property interest belongs to you. If you started with ten tenants (co-owners) and you survive all of them, you now own the entire property! In many cases a JTWRS provides automatic estate planning. In the case of property owned between spouses where each wishes to pass the entire property to the surviving spouse, transfer strategies need to be employed. The property will pass by law to the surviving spouse; a will or other estate planning document has no effect. However, other assets in the estate may be passed by a will or other methods structured into the estate plan.

Property passing by JTWRS has an additional built-in feature—this type of ownership generally avoids probate proceedings until the death of the surviving tenant or co-owner.

◆ **WARNING**   Although the JTWRS has some specific advantages in certain estate planning applications, it can also be a big mistake. If you want assets to pass to people other than joint tenants or co-owners, the JTWRS can prevent you from accomplishing this.

In larger estates tax planning may be a key issue. Using the allowable exemptions or each spouse's individual unified credit ($600,000) to maximize the amount allowed to pass without death tax can be foiled by JTWRS ownership. The cost of this mistake can create up to $250,000 in death tax that is unnecessary and avoidable if proper ownership is accomplished.

*I*n our practice one of the largest problems we see is incorrect ownership, even in cases where clients have established elaborate estate plans. ♦

In our practice one of the largest problems we see is incorrect ownership, even in cases where clients have established elaborate estate plans. This problem might be one of the most costly as well as one of the easiest to remedy.

JTWRS property is specifically titled as right of survivorship and is usually spelled out in the title. If right of survivorship is not clearly stated, tenancy in common is generally assumed.

Tenancy by the Entirety

Tenancy by the entirety is a special type of joint ownership that exists only between spouses. This type of ownership provides for only two owners: husband and wife. Property is deemed to be owned equally by each spouse as long as both are alive. Under this type of ownership, property passes by right of survivorship to the surviving spouse.

A primary difference between JTWRS and tenancy by the entirety is that in tenancy by the entirety, neither spouse may dispose or convey an interest in the property without the consent of the other spouse.

Tenancy in Common

Tenancy in common contains no right of survivorship. Each owner may dispose of his or her interest without regard to the other co-owners. At the time of death, the owner's interest passes by will or the laws of intestacy (without a will) set forth by state statute. The co-owners have no automatic or survivorship rights to the decendent's share of the property.

Tenants in common may hold unequal shares. One tenant may hold a 30 percent interest, and a second tenant may hold the balance or 70 percent of the property. There is no limit on the number of tenants in common. Each owns a percentage or fraction of the undivided total property.

The instrument that conveys ownership of tenancy in common property usually spells out percentages in unequal tenancy. If shares are equally owned by the tenants, the instrument should state "equally as tenants in common."

Community Property

Nine states utilize community property laws: Arizona, California, Idaho, Louisiana, Nevada, New Mexico, Texas and Washington. Wisconsin is not a true community property state but has brought forth legislation that closely resembles that of other community property states. The other 42 states base property ownership on common law principals.

Understanding community property ownership, as well as other forms of ownership, is vital to effective estate planning. The value of a community property asset is different from that of an asset held fee simple or as tenants in common.

Community property deals with property specifically acquired during marriage. This type of ownership assumes that each spouse owns a one-half or equal interest, regardless of the employment status of each spouse or specifically which spouse paid for the property. Under community property law, it is assumed that each spouse owns the property equally. Income generated from community property assets is deemed to be owned equally between each spouse. At the death of one spouse, community property is valued in the estate at 50 percent of the date-of-death value.

Contribution in acquiring the property is assumed to be equal by both spouses. At the death of one spouse, only one-half of the property may be disposed of by the deceased spouse's will. This one-half passes to the surviving spouse only if specific provisions are made to do so.

Because community property deals only with property acquired during marriage, property acquired before marriage by either person remains separate property. Another exception is property that is acquired during marriage in the form of a gift. Property received by one spouse after marriage by gift or inheritance remains separate property.

*T*he most important legislation took place in 1981, when Congress passed the Economic Recovery Tax Act (ERTA). ♦

Community property retains its status as community property even if the individuals move to a non-community-property state. It is extremely important to know how this property is treated, regardless of which state you reside in. The federal government recognizes the rights of each state. This is addressed in the Tenth Amendment to the U.S. Constitution.

PROVISIONS CREATED BY ERTA

In an effort to treat all states equally with regard to estate taxation, the federal government passed several laws starting in 1948. However, the most important legislation took place in 1981, when Congress passed the Economic Recovery Tax Act (ERTA). This act contained sweeping reform in the federal estate and gift tax law. Among other changes, ERTA created provisions for a spouse to leave all property (unlimited amounts) to a surviving spouse with no tax liability. This is referred to as the **unlimited marital deduction.** ERTA also made provisions for a spouse to make *unlimited lifetime gifts* to a spouse free of gift tax. Later we will focus on these two changes and the significant advantages they provide in planning your estate.

◆ **WARNING**   Under ERTA, the benefits provided for individuals living in community property states were significantly improved or enhanced. If this circumstance applies to you, we strongly urge you to review your estate plan. Significant tax savings strategies are available that previously did not exist.

Figure 4.1 summarizes the most common forms of ownership and title.

FIGURE 4.1 The Most Common Forms of Ownership and Title

Ownership and Title Summary

Outright Ownership
1. *Fee Simple*   You own 100 percent outright.
                           You are free to
                           • gift the property,
                           • sell the property or
                           • direct who will receive the
                             property at death.

Joint Ownership
1. *Joint Tenancy*   You own all property
                           with others.
                           You are free to
                           • gift your interest or
                           • sell your interest. You
                             cannot pass your interest at
                             death.

2. *Tenancy by Entirety*   Exists between husband and
                           wife only.
                           There are only two owners.
                           Both are equal owners.
                           The survivor gains full
                           ownership.

3. *Tenancy in Common*   You own part of the property.
                           There can be unequal owners.
                           You are free to
                           • sell your interests,
                           • leave your interest at death
                             or
                           • gift your interest.

4. *Community property*   You own 50 percent.
                           Exists between spouses only.
                           You may pass your interest at
                           death.

CHAPTER 5

Passing Property: Wills

Are Wills Enough?

Property passes in one of three ways at time of death:

1. By will
2. By contract or trust
3. By operation of law

THE WILL—A MISUNDERSTOOD TOOL

A **will** is a simple document that gives instructions pertaining to how assets are to pass to heirs at time of death. Wills are functionless during the course of one's life and have no effect until a person dies. The will passes property that is excluded from passing by operation of law or by contract or trust.

A further examination of wills yields additional aspects that need to be addressed by many families with minor children. A will can make provisions for the following situations:

- *The personal representative:* Wills can determine who will act for you after your death (your *executor*). This person will have many duties to perform. The most important duties include the administration of your estate, distribution of assets to beneficiaries, payment of debts, filing income tax returns, filing estate tax returns (Form 706), payment of taxes and expenses and the collection of life insurance proceeds and retirement benefits.

- *Guardianship:* One of the most important aspects of a will is naming a guardian or guardians for minor children. Most people assume that family members will automatically be allowed to function as guardians for their children. However, most states have specific laws that apply to guardianship. Most problems can be avoided by naming specific guardians in your will. Additionally, the selection of these individuals can be changed when necessary.

- *Testamentary trusts:* A testamentary trust creates provisions that continue after your death (e.g., continued needs or support for minor children or aging parents). The testamentary trust provision in a will can create trusts to hold liquid assets (cash or equivalent) to provide continued income to minor children or others who have long-term needs that trust provisions can accomplish after your death.

During a person's lifetime, the provisions of the will remain private. However, upon death a will becomes public record when it is registered with the court. As such, the contents of a will are available to anyone who makes an inquiry. Those involved in business may be the most adversely affected; debts and asset holdings can become subject to public scrutiny.

Because wills do not hold title to property, many people face multiple probate systems at death. Consider the person who is domiciled in one state and owns real estate in one or more additional states. At death this person's estate is subject to probate in all states where he or she owns real estate. This can cause severe estate settlement complications and needless costs.

*B*ecause a will takes effect only at death, it offers no lifetime benefits. ♦

Because a will takes effect only at death, it offers no lifetime benefits. So ask yourself this question: Have you made absolute provisions for the management of your physical and financial well-being if you become disabled? We were all born unable to care for ourselves and required complete care by our parents or guardians for many years until we could take care of ourselves. But adult disability often requires complete care by others. The difference is that we now have both assets and our physical well-being that need to be managed.

Often clients disclose to us that their estate plans are complete. Many of these individuals have completed wills and assume all their property will pass under the terms of their wills. However, when we examine property in each estate and further determine how it is owned or titled, many of our clients find that these wills cannot accomplish the objectives they set out to achieve.

FIGURE 5.1 Summary of Advantages and Disadvantages of Wills

Advantages

1. They direct assets that pass by will to beneficiaries.

2. They name guardians for minor children.

3. They name personal representatives to settle estates.

4. They may create trusts at death to accomplish postdeath planning.

Disadvantages

1. They take effect only at death.

2. They provide no lifetime planning.

   - There are no provisions for your disability.
   - There are no provisions to name a guardian for you.
   - There is no system for the management of your assets during your lifetime.

3. They are subject to probate.

4. They become public at death.

5. They are ineffective interstate planning tools.

W e generally use wills in simple es- tates where assets are limited. ♦

We generally use wills in simple estates where assets are limited. Estates that contain numerous assets, hold business interests, own property in other states, face multiple probate systems and have children from previous marriages often require additional planning tools, such as trusts. Furthermore, estates that are in excess of $600,000 often benefit from tax planning that trusts can offer versus simple will planning. We will examine these issues in later chapters when we review taxation and trusts.

Wills often have little effect on how assets pass because assets may pass by operation of law or contract. In many applications wills are not sufficient to provide proper planning. By following the estate planning process, use of tools—wills, trusts and so on—can be determined. The effectiveness and timeliness of a will can be summed up in Figure 5.1 In essence, a will should be the only estate planning vehicle when the estate is valued at less than $150,000.

CHAPTER 6

Passing Property: Contracts, Trusts and Operation of Law
The Beneficiary Designation

A basic example of assets that pass by contract are life insurance policies, annuities, individual retirement accounts (IRAs), employee benefit programs and other qualified retirement plans. These contracts often name individuals as beneficiaries. Upon death, the value (proceeds) of these contracts passes directly to those named individuals. A will does not affect the passing of these proceeds unless the will is the named beneficiary.

EXAMPLES OF CONTRACTS

Life Insurance Policies

For example, most of us own life insurance policies. If your estate consists solely of a large life insurance policy (a contract) with specific designated beneficiaries, the entire estate at death passes under the terms of the insurance contract to the stated beneficiaries. Any will that exists has no effect on how or to whom the insurance proceeds will pass. However, if you name your estate as beneficiary, the entire proceeds of the insurance contract will pass to the individuals named in or pass under the provisions of the will. If no will exists, the proceeds are distributed by statutory guidelines set forth by the state in which you reside.

Trust Agreements

Another example of a contract is a trust agreement. A **trust** is a contract between a **grantor** or **settlor** (the person or persons who create the trust) and a **trustee** or **trustees** (persons or entities who hold legal title to property in the trust until the trust provides for distribution).

With a trust, beneficiaries are predetermined by the grantor. ♦

With a trust, beneficiaries are predetermined by the grantor. These beneficiaries are usually entitled to trust assets in a manner set forth under the terms of the trust. Trusts can make distributions to beneficiaries during the lifetime of the grantor but usually distribute property at the death of the grantor. Common examples include income and principal, both of which can be distributed in a variety of ways as set forth under the terms of the trust agreement. Beneficiaries are not parties to the trust agreement but hold an equitable interest in the trust property, commonly referred to as the **corpus.**

OPERATION OF LAW

Earlier we discussed types of ownership where the surviving co-owner or co-owners succeeded to full ownership at the death of other tenants. Property passes by operation of law in one of two ways.

Passing Property by Title

The first deals with how property is titled. An example of property passing in this regard is property that is titled jointly with another person and a right of survivorship exists. This is commonly referred to as joint tenancy with right of survivorship (JTWRS). This type of ownership is often associated with property held between spouses. At the death of one owner, the surviving joint owner or owners succeed to total ownership of the property by law. A common example of an asset that passes by joint tenancy with right of survivorship is a residence titled jointly between spouses. At death the residence passes to the surviving spouse under operation of law by right of survivorship. This also applies to property that is held under tenancies by the entirety.

Intestate Death

The second way that property passes by operation of law is defined when an individual dies without a will; in other words, he or she dies **intestate.** A good example of intestacy is the

We have often wondered how much money . . . is distributed by each state to statute beneficiaries because people do not plan for the distribution of their own estates! ♦

person who owns a residence outright—fee simple. This person may be a widow or widower. If he or she dies intestate, the residence will pass by state law or statute that prescribes how the property will be distributed.

State laws generally provide for distribution of property to next of kin. Percentages and provisions for others, such as surviving spouses, vary from state to state. We have often wondered how much money (property, etc.) is distributed by each state to statute beneficiaries because people do not plan for the distribution of their own estates!

Dower and Curtesy Provisions

In most states there are specific provisions that protect a spouse from being disinherited by the other spouse. These are referred to as **dower** and **curtesy** interests. Most often the surviving spouse is entitled to a certain percentage of the deceased spouse's estate. This is usually no less than one-third to one-half of the estate or probated assets. Thus, in the event that a spouse leaves all property to a third party under a will, such as children or other family members, state law allows the surviving spouse to elect against the will and collect a percentage of the property according to state law.

As previously stated, depending on the type of property, such as life insurance that passes by contract or joint tenancy property that passes by operation of law, quite often people die with property not covered by either of these definitions. We recommend that people be familiar with how their state of domicile will distribute property if they die intestate or with no estate plan in place.

CHAPTER 7

Probate

The Unnecessary Last Resort

Assets that do not pass by contract or survivorship (law) are distributed based on the laws of intestacy and are administered under a system called **probate**. Furthermore, if you die with a will (**testate**), those assets that pass under the terms of your will are also probate assets and are subject to the probate system established in your state.

Figure 7.1 depicts typical examples of property passing under state intestacy laws, which vary from state to state.

Note that this figure is greatly simplified for illustration purposes only. An additional point to consider is the passing of property further down the family or *bloodline*.

PROPERTY THAT PASSES BY BLOODLINE

There are two lines that direct most intestacy laws in the distribution of assets among heirs: (1) **per stirpes** and (2) **per capita**.

Per Stirpes Distribution

Per stirpes is representative of distribution by *line of descent*. If a person dies with two children and one of the children has predeceased the decedent and leaves behind two children (grandchildren of the decedent), the decedent's surviving child receives one-half of the per stirpes distribution and the two grandchildren receive the other half. Thus, each grandchild

FIGURE 7.1 Typical Examples of How Property Passes Under State Intestacy Laws

Widow or widower with one or more children	100% to children
Married, no children	75% to spouse 25% to parents
Married with one child	50% to spouse 50% to child
Married with two or more children	⅓ to spouse ⅔ to children
Unmarried, no children	100% to parents, brothers and sisters equally

Note: Most state intestacy laws make additional provisions to pass property to heirs in the event that the above beneficiaries have predeceased the decedent.

receives a one-fourth interest in the decedent's intestate property.

Per Capita Distribution

Per capita distribution is representative of an equal distribution among a group of named individuals or beneficiaries. Family relationship or kinship has no bearing on this type of distribution. If a parent, son, granddaughter and aunt are beneficiaries, they will all receive equal distributions of the decedent's property.

OTHER LINES OF DISTRIBUTION

What about distributions to adopted children, illegitimate children, posthumous children (children born after a parent's death) and half brothers and half sisters? How are they treated in intestate circumstances?

Adopted Children

Adopted children usually take a full child's share of property. In almost all states an adopted child has the same right to share in the parents' estate as the full child.

Illegitimate Children

Illegitimate children share in property differently between mother and father. In most states the illegitimate child is in the same position as a legitimate child in regard to his or her mother and bloodline relatives. Thus, an illegitimate child will take a grandchild's share of the estate of a maternal grandmother or grandfather. However, this is not true in the case of the father. An illegitimate child will share in the property of the deceased father equal to a normal child's share if the father eventually marries the mother, the father is determined to be the natural father by a court or the father confirms the child as his own.

Posthumous Children

Posthumous children are those born after the death of a parent. They generally are treated as normal children and receive a full child's share.

Half Brothers and Sisters

Half brothers and half sisters have only one parent in common. Most states treat them as normal blood children. In other words, these children receive a whole share.

WHAT HAPPENS TO PROPERTY WHEN NO HEIRS EXIST?

You may wonder what happens to property when there are no heirs. This is commonly referred to as *escheat*. In most states when there are no heirs, the decedent's property passes to the state, or the property "escheats" to the state.

When there is an unmarried person with no children, 100 percent of the property passes to parents, brothers and sisters equally. However, what happens if there are no surviving parents, brothers or sisters? In these cases intestacy laws usually provide for assets to pass to nieces and nephews equally. If there are no nieces or nephews, the property can then pass to grandparents, aunts and uncles. If none of these people survive, the state inherits the property.

If this is your situation, you should investigate the intestacy laws in your own state for an accurate picture of intestacy succession.

FIGURE 7.2 Functions of the Probate Process

- Appoint a probate agent (*administrator*) if there is no will.
- Interpret the will.
- Inventory and assess the value of all property.
- Locate and identify heirs.
- Identify and settle outstanding liabilities and creditors.
- Resolve conflicts between the estate and other parties.
- Complete and file various tax returns.
- Distribute all property.

THE PROBATE SYSTEM: ITS FUNCTIONS AND DISADVANTAGES

The probate system incorporates courts in most counties of each state. The primary function of the probate court and the probate system is to pass property of deceased individuals to heirs. Probate functions both for those who die with a will and for those who die without a will.

As previously mentioned, probate has some definite disadvantages:

- Probate proceedings are public.
- Probate can be very costly.
- Probate can prolong settlement of an estate indefinitely.
- Heirs may be entirely cut off or may be prevented from inheriting property on a timely basis.

The probate system is fairly broad based in settling estates. Not only does the probate system distribute assets to heirs; it is also responsible for a number of other functions. (See Figure 7.2.)

*I*f one of your objectives is to avoid probate, there are several ways to position your estate to accomplish this goal. ♦

Quite frankly, we don't understand why anyone with a moderate accumulation of assets ($150,000 and up) would choose to have their estate probated. In the case of small estates or estates where all heirs or family members have predeceased, individuals may lack the motive to arrange their estates to avoid the probate process. However, if one of your objectives is to avoid probate, there are several ways to position your estate to accomplish this goal. Most of the following techniques involve proper ownership and titling:

- Title property joint tenancy with right of survivorship (JTWRS).

- Create and fund an **inter vivos** or **living trust.**

- Use correct designations of beneficiaries of life insurance and employee benefit programs.

- If you live in a state that has adopted the **uniform probate code,** you can use a designation on bank accounts known as **payable on death** or **POD.**

HOW JTWRS AFFECTS THE PROBATE PROCESS

In Chapter 4 we discussed that property titled joint tenancy with right of survivorship (JTWRS) succeeds by operation of law to the surviving joint tenant. This type of property is not subject to probate or probate proceedings.

However, JTWRS can create several problems. For example, consider property held in this manner between spouses. At the death of the first spouse, the property passes to the surviving spouse. However, unless the surviving spouse retitles the property, it will become a probate asset at the survivor's death.

But what happens if the surviving spouse is unable to retitle the property? Serious problems can arise in situations of simultaneous death, advanced age of the survivor or senility. Under these circumstances retitling is improbable, and property ownership between spouses under JTWRS provisions become *ineffective.*

JTWRS delays probate at the death of the first spouse, but assets titled in this manner become probate assets upon the death of the surviving spouse. If there are more than two tenants or in situations that involve tenants other than spouses, the surviving tenant succeeds to full ownership. Unless this person retitles the asset at the death of the first owner, it will become a probate asset. Furthermore, if you (the surviving spouse) retitle assets with your children, you then subject your assets to risk due to confiscation by your children's creditors, divorce proceedings brought by their spouses and lawsuits that pertain to their negligence.

PROPERTY THAT PASSES BY CONTRACT

In Chapter 6 we examined property that passes by contract (e.g., life insurance policies) as well as employee benefit programs (e.g., pension and profit-sharing plans containing beneficiary designations). It is important to remember that if named persons are designated beneficiaries of these contracts at death, the proceeds will pass directly to these named individuals and avoid probate. However, if the contract designates your "estate" as beneficiary, the contract proceeds will become probate assets at death subject to the provisions of your will. If you die intestate, these assets will pass by state statutes.

One important aspect to consider when choosing beneficiaries with contracts are *minors*. If you elect minor children as beneficiaries, the proceeds from these contracts will become probate assets. Minors are subject to legal guardianship until they become of age. Legal age (usually age 18) varies from state to state. If you have minor children, you must consider the use of trusts (see Chapters 15 and 16) to name guardians and trustees to distribute assets to minors. Making your trust the beneficiary of a contract avoids probate and facilitates distribution of assets to minor children in a systematic mode. Wills can provide for guardians of minor children and can also create trusts at death to distribute assets to your minor children. But remember that assets that pass under your will are probate assets and are fully subject to probate procedures and costs. This is a major factor when trying to decide whether to pass assets by will or by trust.

THE UNIFORM PROBATE CODE

Several states have adopted a Uniform Probate Code. If you reside in one of these states, you may profit from an additional technique to avoid probate that resembles assets that pass by contract. Specifically, certificates of deposit, savings accounts and checking accounts can provide a beneficiary designation that avoids probate. The beneficiary designation is termed *payable on death* or *POD*.

When these accounts are set up, you will usually have the option of choosing a POD designation. If you are fortunate to reside in a state that has adopted this code and have elected to use this feature on your accounts, you must exercise caution where minor children are concerned. The same problems with making minors beneficiaries of life insurance and employee benefit plans hold true for POD designations on bank accounts. *Never use minors for these designations.* Instead, name a responsible adult or a trust that divides the property according to its terms.

The following 18 states have adopted the Unified Probate Code:

Alabama	Minnesota
Alaska	Montana
Arizona	Nebraska
Colorado	New Jersey
Florida	New Mexico
Hawaii	North Dakota
Idaho	South Carolina
Maine	Texas
Michigan	Utah

More states are considering adoption of this code. You should check with your state's probate system to see whether the code has been elected or is being considered.

USING TRUSTS TO AVOID PROBATE

*T*rusts solve problems that no other forms of title or ownership can accomplish. ♦

The use of the inter vivos or living trust to avoid probate and reduce estate tax will be detailed in Chapter 15. It's important to keep in mind that trusts solve problems that no other forms of title or ownership can accomplish. As an example, consider the case of a husband and wife who own all of their assets jointly with right of survivorship. As previously illustrated, these assets are nonprobate assets. At the death of the first spouse, the surviving spouse will succeed to complete ownership—fee simple—by right of survivorship. When this happens, the assets become probate assets upon the survivor's death.

If a husband and wife simply retitle all assets as tenants in common and each tenant titles his or her share under their respective trusts, the assets will escape probate regardless of who dies first or second. The survivor is assured of nonprobate assets. If property is left outright to the surviving spouse as tenant in common, the surviving spouse can retitle the property to his or her trust to avoid probate at his or her death.

Regardless of the size and scope of your assets, the living trust can be used to avoid probate for 100 percent of your property as well as solve numerous other issues that will be detailed in later chapters. Although other techniques are applicable in estate planning, we feel that in most cases trusts are an essential part of the basic format.

THE IMPACT OF TAXATION

In previous discussions we categorized estate planning into three phases: (1) objectives, (2) format and (3) execution.

Most people have some idea of their objectives or what they would like their estate plan to accomplish before they consult an estate planning professional. A few know precisely what they want to accomplish. The main obstacles that we encounter are lack of motivation, lack of knowledge and not knowing who to turn to for direction. All of this creates procrastination.

But one factor that motivates many to take action is taxation. When you finally realize that a major portion of your estate will be confiscated by the federal government through death taxes, you become determined to avoid this eventuality if at all possible.

Consider the individual who has an estate of $2 million. If he or she assumes that he or she can pass the entire estate to a child or grandchild, or anyone for that matter, he or she obviously is not acquainted with "Uncle Sam's plan." The IRS's plan is to collect about 30 percent, or approximately $600,000, before anyone receives anything. Furthermore, the IRS will require its share within nine months of the date of death, in cash. Tax ramifications are clearly the most planned-for aspect of estate planning.

Consider for a moment the following potential dilemmas that estate taxation creates when planning your estate:

- How will assets pass to an heir if they first have to be converted to cash to pay the estate tax liability, assuming there are not enough liquid (cash) assets to pay the tax directly.

- If your primary asset is a business, can the business continue to operate if it has to sell stock or assets to pay your death tax?

- If your estate will be responsible for providing income to disabled children, will estate taxation impact this liability?

If a formal written estate analysis is developed from a clear and accurate picture of how assets are titled and an accurate valuation is placed on each asset, you will be able to realize the impact this onerous confiscatory tax can have on your estate.

A professionally drafted plan should contain strategies to reduce death taxes, to the extent they can be reduced, and offset and pay death taxes. The tools that are commonly used to plan for death taxation will be a primary focus in Part II.

CHAPTER 8

Estate Taxation

The Last Big Surprise

Most often, people are under the impression that because they have paid income tax throughout their lifetimes, at death, taxes stop. In fact, and often to our dismay, we must inform clients about the cruelest tax of all, the **death tax** or **federal estate tax.** In many circumstances the largest beneficiary isn't family or other intended heirs; it is the federal government.

The federal estate tax has undergone many revisions since it was introduced in 1916. The maximum rate when the tax was first passed was approximately 10 percent—rather insignificant in comparison to today's rates!

The Tax Reform Act of 1976 combined the federal estate and the federal gift tax laws. The two are now referred to as the *unified estate and gift tax.* The tax rates are now the same. In other words, if a person gives away $1 million before death, the tax on this gift is identical to the federal estate tax paid if the same $1 million is transferred to others upon death.

In previous chapters we discussed the importance of the formal written estate analysis. It is the key to determining a format for an effective estate plan. One focus of the estate analysis is to calculate death taxes. Our clients always react with the same horror and dismay when they find out what their potential death tax liability is.

Death tax is really a tax the U.S. government places on the right to transfer assets or property held by an individual to other people at the time of his or her death. The tax is formally titled *federal estate tax* and is a transfer tax. We refer to this tax as the cruelest tax because it is capable of confiscating up to 55 percent of your estate. For the ultrawealthy ($10 million

*O*ur clients always react with the same horror and dismay when they find out what their death tax liability will be. ♦

41

and up), it will confiscate up to 60 percent. Some assets are subject to taxation beyond amounts of 70 to 75 percent. In Chapter 12 we will focus on individual retirement accounts and other qualified retirement plans wherein these assets are subject to much greater estate tax rates as well as income taxation.

CHANGES CAUSED BY ERTA

Prior to the Economic Recovery Tax Act of 1981 (ERTA) and prior to 1976, only $60,000 of an estate was exempt from taxation. In 1976 the Tax Reform Act (TRA '76) revised this amount and amortized it up through 1981 to include an exemption of $175,625. This was commonly referred to as the *exemption equivalent* and of course was the tax-free amount that one could exclude from federal estate taxation.

In 1981 ERTA revised the exemption and made some additional sweeping changes:

- It amortized an increase of the exemption to a maximum of $600,000 in 1987.

- It introduced the unlimited marital deduction.

- It restructured the tax rates.

ERTA currently provides you with a $600,000 exemption. The full $600,000 exemption took effect in 1987 and continues today. The history of change to include the current tax rates are as follows:

Year	Exemption
1982	$225,000
1983	275,000
1984	325,000
1985	400,000
1986	500,000
1987 and after	600,000

While Congress has left the exemption alone for the past few years, there is growing concern that it will make some changes in the near future in an effort to fund the health care initiative. (These proposed changes will be further explored in later chapters.)

At the end of 1986 the exemption grew to $600,000 and has remained at this level. The exemption can actually be restated as a tax credit of $192,800. This is the amount of actual tax that is exempt or saved by using your $600,000 exemption.

The second change that came about with ERTA was the introduction of the *unlimited marital deduction*. This provision makes possible two key planning opportunities for married persons by providing the following:

1. The unlimited deduction means that one spouse, or the first spouse to die, can leave as much property as possible to the surviving spouse without any tax liability. Thus, in spousal situations and if planned properly, the federal estate tax liability can be delayed until the death of the surviving spouse.

2. ERTA provides that spouses can gift during their lifetimes as much property to each other or make unlimited gifts to each other without incurring any gift tax consequences.

The third change implemented by ERTA was the restructuring of the actual tax rates. In 1993 ERTA changed the top gift and estate tax rate to 50 percent for estates of $2.5 million to $10 million. For estates over $10 million, the rate reflected the phaseout of the unified credit by imposing an additional tax of 5 percent. The law taxed estates and gifts of $10 million up to $18.34 million at 55 percent. Estates over $18.34 million were to be taxed at 50 percent.

In the preface of this book we referred to the tax act that was passed in mid-1993. The Clinton administration introduced and passed in mid-1993 the Revenue Reconciliation Act of 1993. Essentially this act reinstated pre-1993 estate and gift tax rates. It dissolved the lesser rate that was in effect at the start of 1993 and reinstated the higher pre-1993 rates. This became effective for decedents dying or for gifts made after December 31, 1993.

Under the 1993 Act the estate and gift tax rate on taxable transfers over $2.5 million is 53 percent. The estate and gift tax rate on taxable transfers over $3 million is 55 percent. Under the pre-1993 tax law the unified credit was phased out for estates that exceeded $10 million. This was accomplished by an increase in tax of 5 percent for estates of $10 million but not exceeding $21.04 million ($18.34 million was substituted for $21.04 million in the case of decedents dying and for gifts made after 1992). The 1993 Tax Act changed this phaseout plan by deleting the requirement that $18.34 million be substituted for $21.04 million in computing the increased tax on post-1992 transfers that exceed $10 million.

In summary, the tax rates that were proposed under ERTA, which would have been in effect for 1993 and would have been less, have been repealed and are back to the higher pre-1993 rates. We think the next few years and the current health care reform in view will prove to be very interesting with regard to potential changes in the estate and gift taxes.

The rates in the following table summarize the changes that ERTA produced:

Taxable Estate	1981 Tax	1993 Tax
$ 500,000	$ 108,800	$ 0
1,000,000	298,800	153,000
1,500,000	508,800	363,000
2,000,000	733,800	588,000
2,500,000	978,850	833,000
3,000,000	1,243,800	1,098,000
5,000,000	2,503,800	2,198,000

These rates reflect the credit of the tax equivalent of the $600,000 exemption or $192,800.

ASSET DISTRIBUTION AND TAX PLANNING

The devastating ramification of death tax has segmented estate planning into two general areas:

1. Planning for asset distribution (*dispositive*) or who gets what

2. Tax planning

For people who have property cumulatively valued at over $600,000, integration of distribution and tax planning go hand in hand.

Example

Linden has an estate of $1 million. How can she plan for distribution when a tax of approximately $153,000 is due before any assets can be distributed to heirs? Consider also that Linden has one primary asset—real estate. How does her estate pay the tax liability without being forced to sell the property? The selling of the real estate may adversely affect her planning objectives and most likely will not be done in the best interest of either party. The only entity that will benefit will be the federal government.

---

*T*ax planning is an integral part of estate planning and in most estates is the single largest factor to contend with before dispositive provisions can be structured. ♦

Tax planning is an integral part of estate planning and in most estates is the single largest factor to contend with before dispositive provisions can be structured. Remember that federal estate tax is charged on the right to transfer property. However, the tax is applied and calculated on the asset value of the transfer. In other words, the tax is derived from the value of the property transferred. The tax is also all-encompassing and is levied from the total value of all property in your name at your death. The following are the only current exceptions:*

- Social Security benefits based on your life now payable to your beneficiaries.

- Life insurance proceeds on your life, if you have no right of ownership.

- Death benefit only plans created by employers. These proceeds pass directly to designated beneficiaries and must meet certain IRS guidelines to qualify.

- Money that passes directly to named beneficiaries from certain annuity purchases sponsored by employers. These annuity payments also have to be structured to meet specific IRS guidelines.

Life Insurance

One asset that remains a great consumer dilemma is life insurance.

Most people are under the impression that life insurance is not a taxable asset. Many have been told by their insurance agents that life insurance proceeds pass tax-free to beneficiaries. While this is in part true, it is not the complete story.

Named beneficiaries do receive life insurance proceeds free of income tax. However, these proceeds are first fully included in the gross estate of the deceased individual if the individual *owns* the insurance contracts and are subject to estate taxes. We distinctly recall a case in which we explained this issue to a physicist who owned a $2 million life insurance policy. He

---

* A few other interests affect only a small number of people, but they are beyond the scope of this publication.

Most people are under the impression that life insurance is not a taxable asset. . . . While this is in part true, it is not the complete story. ♦

vehemently argued with us when we revealed to him that his $2 million policy was worth only approximately $1 million after being included in his estate and undergoing estate tax. He stated that his agent told him it would be paid to his beneficiaries tax-free. Income-tax-free, yes. Estate-tax-free, *no!*

It is clear that as with any asset or property an individual owns at his or her time of death, life insurance contracts are fully included for federal estate taxation. However, life insurance proceeds are received income-tax-free by a decedent's estate and are not subject to income tax when received by a beneficiary.

Understanding the correct tax liability and the amount of insurance owned by an individual can be a key factor to accomplishing an effective estate plan. Consider an individual with a $2 million estate. If $1 million of the estate property is a life insurance contract (or contracts) and this individual assumes that the insurance will pass estate-tax-free to a beneficiary, this becomes a very costly mistake. Let's examine why.

From our previous example we know that the approximate total tax on the estate of an individual who transfers $1 million is approximately $148,000. Adding an additional $1 million to the estate escalates the tax liability to approximately $583,000. More than double! How can this be? The following two things have occurred:

1. The size of the estate has increased and therefore so does the total tax liability.

2. The extra $1 million included in the estate because of the inclusion of the insurance has pushed the estate tax rate from approximately 37 percent to 45 percent. The first $1 million is inclusive of the total estate ($2 million) and is taxed at the higher rate.

To fully understand what has happened, let's look at the actual federal estate and gift tax rates shown in Figure 8.1. The federal estate tax rate currently starts at 37 percent and escalates to a maximum of 55 percent for each dollar of value in an estate between $600,000 and $10 million. While it is stated that the tax rates start at 37 percent, the tax table reflects rates as low as 18 percent. This may appear to be confusing, but remember that the first $600,000 passes tax-free under the unified credit for each person's estate. The rates in Figure 8.1 are before the $600,000 exemption is applied.

To find out what the actual tax is on $600,000, find the column in Figure 8.1 that reflects an estate over $500,000 but not over $750,000. The tax on $500,000 is $155,800. The balance, or $100,000, is taxed at 37 percent, or $37,000. Adding

FIGURE 8.1 Federal Estate and Gift Tax Rates (1993 and Beyond)

If Your Tax Base Is Over	But Not Over	Your Tax Is	+ %	On Excess Over
$ 0	$10,000	$ 0	18%	$ 0
10,000	20,000	1,800	20	10,000
20,000	40,000	3,800	22	20,000
40,000	60,000	8,200	24	40,000
60,000	80,000	13,000	26	60,000
80,000	100,000	18,200	28	80,000
100,000	150,000	23,800	30	100,000
150,000	250,000	38,300	32	150,000
250,000	500,000	70,800	34	250,000
500,000	750,000	155,800	37	500,000
750,000	1,000,000	248,300	39	750,000
1,000,000	1,250,000	345,800	41	1,000,000
1,250,000	1,500,000	448,300	43	1,250,000
1,500,000	2,000,000	555,800	45	1,500,000
2,000,000	2,500,000	780,800	49	2,000,000
2,500,000	3,000,000	1,025,800	53	2,500,000
3,000,000	10,000,000	1,290,800	55	3,000,000
10,000,000	21,040,000	5,140,800	60	10,000,000
21,040,000		11,764,800	55	21,040,000

Note: All rates are before the application of the $600,000 unified credit or exemption equivalent. The actual tax credit for each unified credit is $192,800.

Wе are constantly amazed at how many people have not been informed or have not updated their plans to take advantage of the potential tax-saving elements ERTA provides. ♦

the two taxes together gives us a sum of $192,800. Each unified credit can be restated as an actual tax credit of $192,800. If the tax on a $600,000 estate is $192,800 and we apply the unified credit of $192,800, the subsequent tax is zero.

Assuming that we have not used the unified credit or part of it before death, the tax rates reflect a starting rate of 37 percent after applying the full exemption.

In the case of the person who has a $2 million estate, the tax rate on the $2 million is derived from the left-hand column of Figure 8.1 that lists the base as over $1.5 million but not over $2 million. The tax is $555,800 plus 45 percent of the remainder of $2 million or 45 percent of $500,000. Forty-five percent of $500,000 is $225,000. The addition of the tax on $1.5 million plus the additional tax on the balance of the $500,000 totals $780,800. If we credit the tax on the first $600,000 or the tax credit of $192,800, the federal estate tax liability is $588,000.

CURRENT FEDERAL ESTATE TAX LAWS

ERTA significantly changed the way that we now construct and format estate plans. If your plan was completed prior to the passage of ERTA or before September 13, 1981, it may no longer be effective. We are constantly amazed at how many people have not been informed or have not updated their plans to take advantage of the potential tax-saving elements ERTA provides. A review of the current federal estate tax laws provides the following information:

- The federal estate tax is applicable to the fair market value of property.

- It is a tax on the right to transfer property.

- Federal estate tax must be paid in cash nine months from the date of death.

- The tax must be paid before property passes to beneficiaries.

- The tax starts at 37 percent after the application of the unified credit.

- The tax applies to estates that are valued over $600,000.

- The tax code provides for an unlimited amount of property to transfer to a surviving spouse with no taxation even if this is a second or third marriage. (See information on QTIP trust planning in Chapter 16.)

In addition, most of us are familiar with the standard deductions allowed on our income tax returns. The IRS gives each of us deductions that apply to federal estate taxation. These deductions are as follows:

- Debts (e.g., mortgages)

- Expenses incurred in the administration of the estate

- Funeral expenses

- Casualty losses

- Marital deductions

- Charitable deductions

These outlined deductions will be discussed in detail in Chapter 14. The estate and gift tax rates are perhaps the greatest threat to many estates. The rates start at an effective rate of approximately 37 percent for each dollar over the unified credit amount. The rates are subject to change brought about by the need for increased revenues by our government. We have seen small changes made under the Clinton administration, and we can only speculate what future changes will be made as government tackles the deficit and the proposed national health care initiative. Is it any wonder that planning for the tax bite in your estate has become a key planning issue?

CHAPTER 9

States and Death Taxes

Getting Their Fair Share

If you thought death taxes were limited to Uncle Sam's pockets, beware of the state where you reside. States tax individuals at death in three ways:

1. By applying a gap-tax
2. By taxing the estate directly
3. By actual application of an inheritance tax

GAP-TAX STATES

Gap-tax states are referred to as *revenue-sharing states*. These states actually collect taxes that are computed by the federal government in the estate tax computation. Gap-tax states are also commonly referred to as **state death tax credit** states. Regardless of which term is used, these states receive their portion of death taxes from the federal government.

The gap-tax or state death tax credit states are as follows:

Alabama	Florida	New Mexico	Virginia
Alaska	Georgia	North Dakota	Washington
Arizona	Hawaii	Oregon	West Virginia
Arkansas	Idaho	Rhode Island	Wisconsin
California	Illinois	South Carolina	Wyoming
Colorado	Maine	Texas	
District of	Minnesota	Utah	
Columbia	Nevada	Vermont	

FIGURE 9.1 Maximum Credit Allowed for State Death Tax Credit

Adjusted Taxable Estate Equal to or More Than—	Adjusted Taxable Estate Less Than—	Credit on Amount in Col. 1	Rates of Credit on Excess over Amounts in Col. 1
$ 40,000	$ 90,000	$	0.8%
90,000	140,000	400	1.6
140,000	240,000	1,200	2.4
240,000	440,000	3,600	3.2
440,000	640,000	10,000	4.0
640,000	840,000	18,000	4.8
840,000	1,040,000	27,600	5.6
1,040,000	1,540,000	38,800	6.4
1,540,000	2,040,000	70,800	7.2
2,040,000	2,540,000	106,800	8.0
2,540,000	3,040,000	146,800	8.8
3,040,000	3,540,000	190,800	9.6
3,540,000	4,040,000	238,800	10.4
4,040,000	5,040,000	290,800	11.2
5,040,000	6,040,000	402,800	12.0
6,040,000	7,040,000	522,800	12.8
7,040,000	8,040,000	650,800	13.6
8,040,000	9,040,000	786,800	14.4
9,040,000	10,040,000	930,800	15.2
10,040,000		1,082,800	16.0

The tax paid to the gap-tax states is an actual credit against federal estate taxation. This credit is available for adjusted taxable estates that equal or exceed $40,000. The maximum credit allowed is reflected in the table in Figure 9.1.

The federal credit is allowed for the amount of state death tax actually paid, up to the limits of the table in Figure 9.1. A credit estate tax ensures that a state receives total death taxes equal to or exceeding the amount in the table.

ESTATE-TAX STATES

States that tax estates directly are referred to as **estate-tax states.** These states tax estates in a manner similar to the federal government. They apply a tax rate to the net taxable estate.

FIGURE 9.2 State Estate Tax Rates

Net Taxable Estate		Tax Rates	
		Tax on	*Rate on Excess*
From	*To*	*Col. 1*	*(above Col. 1)*
$ 0	$ 50,000	$ 0	5%
50,000	100,000	2,500	7
100,000	200,000	6,000	9
200,000	400,000	15,000	10
400,000	600,000	35,000	11
600,000	800,000	57,000	12
800,000	1,000,000	81,000	13
1,000,000	2,000,000	107,000	14
2,000,000	4,000,000	247,000	15
4,000,000	Balance	547,000	16

States that compute their own death taxes do not share in revenues collected under the federal estate tax revenue-sharing program. ♦

States that compute their own death taxes do not share in revenues collected under the federal estate tax revenue-sharing program. This is the primary difference between gap-tax or state death tax credit states and estate-tax states. Furthermore, states that have a direct estate tax collect a much greater amount of tax. The estate-tax states* are as follows:

Massachusetts

Mississippi

New York

Ohio

Oklahoma

Computation of state estate tax is accomplished by the following method:

- Compute the sum of all property that is subject to the tax.

- Subtract exemptions and deductions to determine the net taxable estate.

- Compute the state estate tax from the tax table.

---

*   Puerto Rico also has an estate tax.

FIGURE 9.3 Example of a State's Beneficiary Classification

Exemptions Class A	Amount of Exemption
Husband or wife	$60,000
Natural, legal or informally adopted child under 18	5,000
Natural or adoptive ancestor, lineal natural adoptive or informally adoptive descendant	2,000
Class B Brother, sister, descendant thereof, wife, widow of son (daughter-in-law), husband or widower of daughter (son-in-law)	500
Class C All others	100

- Subtract any discounts that may apply to arrive at the net tax due.

The tax rates are included in the table in Figure 9.2.

INHERITANCE-TAX STATES

Inheritance-tax states derive their death tax from the value of properties that pass to beneficiaries. Beneficiaries are categorized by various classes. The tax is actually computed on the share each beneficiary receives: hence, the term *inheritance tax*.

Inheritance-tax states base their rates on different classes of beneficiaries. The decedent's closest relatives or blood relations reflect the lowest rates and highest exemptions. The more distant a relative is, the greater the tax rate and the lower the exemption. Spouses generally pay taxes at the lowest rate and usually have the largest exemptions.

Tax rates depend on the size of the inherited property and the classification of the beneficiaries. Tax rates vary depending on your state of domicile. If you live in a state that has an inheritance tax, you should check your state tax tables. The following states are inheritance-tax states:

FIGURE 9.4 Typical Inheritance Tax Rates

Share in Excess of Exemption From	To	Tax on Col. 1	Class A Rate on Excess (above Col. 1)
$ 0	$ 25,000	$ —	1%
25,000	50,000	250	2
50,000	200,000	750	3
200,000	300,000	5,250	4
300,000	500,000	9,250	5
500,000	700,000	19,250	6
700,000	1,000,000	31,250	7
1,000,000	1,500,000	52,250	8
1,500,000	Balance	92,250	10

Share in Excess of Exemption From	To	Tax on Col. 1	Class B Rate on Excess (above Col. 1)
0	100,000	—	7
100,000	500,000	7,000	10
500,000	1,000,000	47,000	12
1,000,000	Balance	107,000	15

Share in Excess of Exemption From	To	Tax on Col. 1	Class C Rate on Excess (above Col. 1)
0	100,000	—	10
100,000	1,000,000	10,000	10
1,000,000	Balance	145,000	20

Connecticut	Michigan
Delaware	Montana
Indiana	Nebraska
Iowa	New Hampshire
Kansas	New Jersey
Kentucky	North Carolina
Louisiana	Pennsylvania
Maryland	South Dakota
	Tennessee

An example of a state's beneficiary classification is illustrated in Figure 9.3. The typical after-exemption tax rates are illustrated in Figure 9.4.

It's important to note that inheritance-tax states also participate and receive funds from the federal estate tax revenue-sharing program.

A few states have separate gift taxes as well as the three categories for federal estate taxation.

It is important when estimating death taxes that you or your estate planner research the laws and tax rates of the state where you reside to determine your correct tax liability. The precise estate tax liability is a primary issue in every estate plan, and should be fully understood when determining the strategies needed to properly plan your estate.

◆ **WARNING**   State death taxes are computed and apply in the state of *domicile* (state you primarily live in). If you live in Colorado and have a winter home in Florida, you will be subject to Colorado's state death tax system. There have been cases where two states have applied their tax systems to the same estate contending that the decedent was domiciled in both states. However, this is not the typical case.

CHAPTER 10

Unification of Estate and Gifting

The Great Marriage

As we have mentioned, in 1976 Congress passed legislation that united the federal estate and the gift tax codes. Under the Tax Reform Act of 1976 (TRA 1976), estates and gifts are now taxed alike. The federal estate tax rates discussed in the previous chapter have identical application to gifts.

The tax system prior to 1976 gave each individual a separate exemption for gifts—namely, $30,000. A separate tax rate for gifts that exceeded the $30,000 exemption was applied. Estates were allowed a $60,000 exemption and also had a separate tax rate above this amount.

THE UNIFIED CREDIT

Today the unification of the federal estate and gift taxes is commonly called the **unified credit** or the **exemption equivalent**. As defined in Chapter 8, this exemption is currently $600,000. It applies to gifts made during the decedent's lifetime, or if not utilized during his or her lifetime, the exemption or balance of the unused portion can be applied as a credit toward estate taxation. As previously illustrated, the actual tax credit is $192,800. This $192,800 is the tax equivalent of $600,000 of assets; or more simply put, the $600,000 exemption can be restated as an actual tax credit of $192,800. To see how the unified credit functions in an actual estate and gift application, consider the following:

Example

Steve, a widower with an estate of $1 million, makes a $200,000 gift to his son in January 1991. Steve then dies in January 1993. At the time Steve makes the $200,000 gift to his son, he files a gift tax return. Neither party pays gift tax. The $200,000 is part of his $600,000 exemption. When Steve dies, he has $400,000 of his exemption remaining.

Using the same example, let's say that Steve gifts his son $700,000 in the same year as the previous example. Steve files a gift tax return. His exemption excludes the first $600,000, and he pays a gift tax of approximately $37,000 on the balance ($100,000) of the gift. The tax is paid in the year the gift is made. The tax on the $100,000 is derived from the estate and gift tax rates. At death, Steve's heirs have no remaining exemption or unified credit to apply to his estate tax calculation.

This example illustrates the unification of gift and estate taxation. While it can be confusing at times, remember that the unified credit and the exemption equivalent are one in the same. Estate planners use both terms freely. When planning your estate it is important to understand the following points about the exemption:

- The $600,000 exemption or unified credit applies to gifts made during one's lifetime or transfers at death (gift tax and estate tax).

- The $600,000 exemption can be restated as an actual tax credit of $192,800.

- The credit can be used partially for gifts made during one's lifetime. The balance is applied against federal estate tax on transfers at death.

THE ANNUAL GIFT TAX EXCLUSION

In addition to the $600,000 lifetime exemption from gift tax or estate tax, the IRS allows each individual the right to make an unlimited number of tax-free small gifts. The amount of these gifts is limited to $10,000 annually per recipient. If a person has one child or a dozen children, the gift can be applied to all.

For example, if a person has two children, he or she may gift to each child $10,000 per year. In addition to these small annual gifts to children, a person can make the same gift to as many unrelated people as desired.

Example

Steve, who has two children and an estate of $1 million, decides to gift each of his children $10,000 in 1993. Steve is able to do this without any effect on his unified credit or exemption equivalent. Furthermore, neither he nor the children have to file a gift tax return, nor do they incur any gift tax.

---

*O*ne of the great family estate planning opportunities involves utilizing the annual gift tax exclusion between spouses to maximize the value of the gifts to children without adverse effect on the remaining unified credit. ♦

This form of gifting is referred to as the **annual gift tax exclusion.** For many years the annual gift tax exclusion was limited to $3,000 per recipient. In 1982 the exclusion was increased to exclude gifts of under $10,000.

One of the great family estate planning opportunities involves utilizing the annual gift tax exclusion between spouses to maximize the value of the gifts to children without adverse effect on the remaining unified credit.

Example

Let's now assume Steve is married. He can combine his gift with his wife; collectively, they can gift each child $20,000 or a total of $40,000 each year. This total of $40,000 has no effect on either Steve's $600,000 lifetime exemption or his spouse's $600,000 exemption.

If Steve and his wife had made gifts in excess of the $40,000 (say, $60,000), the additional $20,000 qualifies for and reduces the unified credit by $20,000 and leaves a balance of $580,000. If Steve is the overcontributor, he is also required to file a gift tax return for the $20,000 over and above his annual exclusion amount. The amount over the gift tax exclusion can also be split between both husband and wife. The couple may both elect to file gift tax returns for $10,000, thus leaving a balance of $590,000 in each remaining unified credit.

The idea of using spouses to share in annual gifts to children is called **gift splitting.** In order for the gift to qualify for a split gift, the other spouse has to agree to share in the gift.

When spouses share in a gift or split a gift, a gift tax return has to be filed in the year the gift is made.

With the advent of the unlimited number of these small annual gifts, a person can conceivably gift his or her estate into a position where no estate tax is applied at death.

If Steve and his spouse have an estate of $1.3 million, they could possibly gift $100,000 to their two children over three years. The first two years they could share in gifts of $40,000 each year, and the third year they could share in a gift of $20,000. If the balance of the estate were split equally or each spouse owned $600,000 and each made provisions to use his or her unified credit or the $600,000 exemption, the balance ($1.2 million) would pass estate-tax-free at death. This arrangement would allow them to keep $1.2 million in the total combined estate for income production during their lifetimes and escape all federal estate tax at death. The $100,000 that had been gifted would of course not be available for their income production. We will explore this planning technique as well as others in later chapters.

A person can gift his or her estate into a position where no estate tax is applied at death. ♦

The couple could also gift $1.3 million (the total value of their estate) in one year. Assuming that they share in gifts, they could jointly gift $20,000 to 65 people and thus eliminate any possible gift tax or estate tax liability from this point forward. This is obviously not an estate planning idea that we would recommend!

♦ WARNING

Many of our clients believe the annual gift tax exclusion applies only to gifts made to their children. The annual gift tax exclusion applies to gifts of $10,000 or under and is unlimited in number as well as recipients. These gifts can be made to perfect strangers—as many as is deemed viable. Thus, you could give your entire estate away in one year by dividing the total estate value by 10,000 and then finding that exact number of people to gift to!

Gifts include not only gifts of cash but also other types of property or assets. It is always advisable to determine what property should be given and when. It is generally more advantageous for one to gift assets that are appreciating so the appreciation will accumulate outside of the estate and not compound the size of the estate which results in greater estate tax liability at death.

SUMMARY

In summary, it is important for each person to understand the following:

- The annual gift tax exclusion is in addition to the $600,000 lifetime gift tax exemption.

- The annual gift tax exclusion is not limited to gifts made to children. Gifts made to any individual or individuals qualify.

- The annual gift tax exclusion is not limited in number. The gift can be made to one person or 100.

- These small gifts are limited to $10,000 each per gift, per year.

- These gifts may be split between spouses. The gift is split if the other spouse agrees to share in the gift. Thus, married persons may gift $20,000 to each recipient, gift-tax-free. A gift tax return is required for gift splitting between spouses.

CHAPTER 11

Transfers at Death
A Stepped-Up Basis

The rules of cost basis often can determine when property should be given. The laws regarding the basis of a gifted asset or an asset transferred at death are quite often misunderstood.

Cost basis in property can be a significant factor when trying to decide whether to gift assets during lifetime or transfer them at death. Let's examine this in more detail.

Cost basis is the value of an asset when acquired. If John Minor purchased a house for $30,000 in 1965, his cost basis in the property is $30,000. However, today (1993) the fair market value of the house is $100,000. If Mr. Minor gifts the house to his son in 1993, his son takes on his father's cost basis in the property. If the son sells the property the following day for $100,000, he will incur capital gains tax on $70,000. The amount of gain is equal to the fair market value ($100,000) less the cost basis ($30,000) carried over from the donor (Mr. Minor).

In this example Mr. Minor is referred to as the **donor,** or the person who makes the gift. His son is referred to as the **donee,** the person who receives the gift. When gifts are made during a donor's lifetime, the donee assumes the cost basis of the donor.

Property transferred at death or **testamentary** receives a **step-up-in-basis** to the date of death value. Beneficiaries receive a basis that reflects the date of death value of the transferred property. If the property is sold for an amount that reflects the date of death value, there will be no capital gains tax liability.

If Mr. Minor leaves the house to his son at death and the house is worth $100,000 the day he dies, his son's basis in the house is "stepped up" to reflect the $100,000. If the son sells the property the next day for $100,000, he will incur no capital gains tax liability.

The amount of tax on the gain of $70,000 is by today's standard very small. However, consider the individual who started a business from scratch that became a booming enterprise! The start-up expenses generally are extremely low, and in some cases there may not be any cost basis. Furthermore, there may actually be a negative cost basis. The current value of stock and business holdings 20 to 30 years later is often in the millions of dollars. How do the owners transfer the value of the business to heirs or others without loss of value due to capital gains, gift or estate tax ramifications? Should they gift stock and business assets during lifetime or wait and transfer assets at death to give heirs a stepped-up basis? We will focus on some of these planning dilemmas in Chapter 20.

SUMMARY

In summary, the following points are critical to estate planning when capital gains property is a large part of the estate:

- A donee takes on the cost basis of the donor for gifts made during the lifetime of the donor.

- The donee assumes the capital gains liability when the asset is sold.

- Assets transferred at death receive a *step-up-in-basis* for the beneficiary to the date-of-death fair market value.

CHAPTER 12

Planning for Mass Tax on IRAs and Other Retirement Plans
The Multiple Tax Trap

When dealing with your retirement plan you need to plan for several potential taxable events. These include the following:

- Income tax on lump sum distributions during your lifetime.

- Regular income tax on your retirement plan funds at your death.

- The 15 percent **excess accumulations estate tax** created to prevent avoidance of the excess distribution tax by persons who minimize lifetime distributions.

- The 15 percent **excess distribution tax** on excess distributions taken during your lifetime. (This is a companion tax to the excess accumulations estate tax.)

INCOME TAX AT DEATH

Income taxation on contributions made to qualified retirement plans is deferred until you actually receive a distribution from the plan. Distributions, when paid out, are taxable to you (the participant) as ordinary income. If you are taking planned distributions (other than lifetime or joint annuity options) and you die before the balance of distributions is paid out or predecease the start of any distributions, your beneficiary must pay tax on the proceeds as ordinary income.

A key planning strategy is to make certain that your spouse is named as the beneficiary to all qualified plan benefits or IRAs. ♦

One exception to this rule is when a beneficiary is the *surviving spouse*. Income tax may continue to be deferred if the plan proceeds are left to the surviving spouse.

A surviving spouse receiving distributions from qualified retirement plans may elect to roll over the distributions to other qualified plans or his or her own individual retirement accounts (IRAs). This rollover will avoid current taxation on the distributed amount if transferred correctly. Any other beneficiary receiving the deceased participant's benefits is not permitted to make a rollover of the distributed amounts, and income taxes must be paid by the recipients (e.g., children). This includes any trusts (revocable or nonrevocable living trusts) contained in the estate plan that are named as the beneficiary.

A key planning strategy is to make certain that your spouse is named as the beneficiary of all qualified plan benefits or IRAs. In the event that plan proceeds pass by any other means to any other people (e.g., children), there will be an immediate income tax liability on the plan proceeds.

Example

Bill Blass is 70 and has $1.5 million in his IRA. He plans on waiting until age 70½ before taking a distribution. However, Bill dies a few days after his 70th birthday, and he designated his revocable living trust the beneficiary of his IRA.

Before the proceeds of his IRA can pass to his surviving spouse, they are first subject to immediate income tax as ordinary income. Bill made a tremendous error in his planning. If Bill had named his spouse as beneficiary, his spouse could have rolled the proceeds from Bill's IRA into her own IRA and avoided an immediate tax on the total IRA amount.

Proceeds from qualified plans paid to a nonspouse beneficiary are subject to current income taxation on the distributed amounts. Immediate tax liability can be reduced by making provisions for the proceeds to be paid out over a period of time to nonspousal beneficiaries in the form of annuity payments.

Most beneficiary designations name the spouse as the first beneficiary with the family trust (B trust) or others as the secondary beneficiaries. The surviving spouse is permitted to roll over the proceeds to an IRA and avoid income tax. The trust or beneficiaries other than a surviving spouse *will not* be able to do so.

In addition to the income tax ramifications at the death of a plan participant, the total accumulated balance is part of and subject to federal estate tax.

In Bill's case, he had $1.5 million in his IRA account. But let's assume that Bill is now a widower or divorced. If he has additional assets of $2 million, for a total gross estate of $3.5 million, his estate will be subject to the 55 percent federal estate tax before deductions. Not only is the estate subject to estate tax; the $1.5 million in the IRA is subject to income tax at his death.

THE 15 PERCENT EXCESS ACCUMULATIONS ESTATE TAX

In addition to possible immediate income tax as well as federal estate tax, Bill Blass may be taxed an additional 15 percent on a portion of his IRA.

Under the Tax Reform Act of 1986 (TRA '86), a new additional estate tax was created to prevent avoidance of the lifetime tax imposed on people who take excessive distributions from their retirement plans. Imposed at death, this tax is in addition to any regular estate tax and is equal to 15 percent of a person's excess retirement accumulations.

Excess retirement accumulations can be defined as the sum of amounts payable under qualified pension, profit sharing, ESOPs and other retirement plans; tax deferred annuities; and IRAs. Once the sum of these benefits is calculated, you then subtract an amount equal to the present value of a $150,000 annuity payable for your life at a given age. Any excess is subject to a flat 15 percent tax.

Figure 12.1 shows the excess accumulations tax on Bill's $1.5 million IRA account. If Bill had $2 million in his IRA at time of death, the excess accumulations tax would be $131,300.

FIGURE 12.1 Excess Retirement Accumulations Worksheet

Transfer date	1/94
Table rate (variable)	7.4%
Total amount payable at death	$1,500,000
Protected annual amount	$150,000
Annuity factor	7.498
Value of protected annuity	$1,124,670
Excess amount subject to 15% tax	$375,330
Excess accumulations tax	*$56,300*

FIGURE 12.2 Potential Losses from Taxes Applicable to IRAs and Pension Lump Sum Distributions at Death

---

Amount in Bill's IRA	$1,500,000

- *Tax 1:* Amounts exceeding $1,124,676 (protected amount) are taxed at a 15% rate; the tax is $56,299.

Amount remaining after excess accumulations tax	$1,443,701

- *Tax 2:* $1,443,701 is subject to federal estate tax. The tax is $721,851.

Amount remaining after federal estate tax	721,850

- *Tax 3:* The GSTT tax, if any, is based on $721,850 less the sum of GSTT tax $0 plus $1,000,000. The 55% rate is applied against –$278,150. The GSTT is $0.

Amount remaining after generation-skipping tax	$721,850

- *Tax 4:* Both the estate tax and the GSTT are deductible in computing the income tax. The 15% $56,299 is not deductible. The income tax on a lump sum of $778,149 is $217,882.

Amount remaining after federal income tax	$ 503,968
Amount Bill started with	1,500,000
Total taxes	996,032
Net amount available to grandson (or heirs)	503,968
Percent remaining	34%
Percent lost	66%

If Bill had $3 million in his IRA at time of death, the excess accumulations tax would be $281,300.

Keep in mind that the excess accumulations tax is in addition to income tax, federal estate tax and **generation-skipping transfer tax (GSTT).** This tax is illustrated further in Chapter 13. The potential loss from the sum of all four taxes applicable to Bill's IRA represents approximately 66 percent. (See Figure 12.2, which assumes that Bill and his spouse die in the same year and the estate transfers to their grandson.)

If Bill had $2 million in his IRA before death, his tax picture would reflect the following values:

Amount Bill started with	$2,000,000
Total taxes	1,364,032
Net amount available to grandson (or heirs)	635,968
Percent remaining	32%
Percent lost	68%

If Bill had $3 million in his IRA before death, his tax picture would reflect these values:

Amount Bill started with	$3,000,000
Total taxes	2,191,840
Net amount available to grandson (or heirs)	808,160
Percent remaining	27%
Percent lost	73%

Keep in mind that these are the balances of the IRA portion of the estate only and do not include the loss on the additional non-IRA assets that make up Bill's estate ($2 million).

We have seen estate cases where as much as 80 percent of retirement plan proceeds is lost to the sum of all four tax liabilities!

The excess accumulations tax cannot be reduced by the estate tax marital deduction. This is true even when the surviving spouse receives the entire plan accumulations. Furthermore, it cannot be reduced by the charitable deduction even if the charity receives the full amount.

One erroneous prevailing concept we have recently heard is the idea that because an estate is small (under $600,000), there will not be any taxes to pay at death. While this is currently true with regard to estate taxes, if your estate has a qualified retirement benefit that will be received as a lump sum by beneficiaries at your death or in the case of spousal estates at the death of the surviving spouse, there may be significant income tax liability. You should be aware of this potential tax liability and integrate it within the overall estate plan.

The unified credit, as well as any other credit, cannot be used to reduce this tax. For example, the credit for taxes paid on prior transfers is not allowed to offset any of the excess accumulations tax. The tax is applicable regardless of the number of beneficiaries named to receive the proceeds. It is impossible to reduce this tax by utilizing multiple beneficiaries. The tax applies on distributions to beneficiaries in the form of lump sums, installment payments and annuity payments.

Payment of the 15 percent excess accumulations tax is the responsibility of your estate. If you anticipate a large accumulation in your retirement plan, you should consider some of the

We have seen cases where as much as 80 percent of retirement plan proceeds is lost to the sum of all four tax liabilities! ♦

One erroneous prevailing concept we have recently heard is the idea that because an estate is small (under $600,000), there will not be any taxes to pay at death. ♦

following planning techniques to offset taxation:

1. *Distributions from plans can be rolled over to IRAs during your lifetime.* The 15 percent tax may be reduced or eliminated if minimum annual distributions fall below the current annual limitation. In the event distributions exceed the limit, rollovers may delay the tax. This depends largely on the level of future income tax rates.

2. *Nonqualified or private pension plans can be elected as alternatives to qualified applicable plans.*

3. *The Technical and Miscellaneous Revenue Act of 1988 (TAMRA '88) made possible the ability for a surviving spouse to elect to defer the excess accumulations tax until his or her death.* However, any payments to a credit shelter trust (family or B trust) or any beneficiary other than the surviving spouse will *not* qualify for the deferral.

4. *Extension of the distribution period.* Election of an annuity (guaranteed fixed monthly income distributions) instead of a lump sum may reduce the tax. Consideration of the time value of money for the family unit will have to be explored to determine if this option is viable. Lately we have witnessed that the majority of our clients elect lump sum distributions from their pension and retirement plans versus taking out an annuity (planned payout) within the guidelines of the plan. The prevailing reason is that most participants feel they can manage their funds and achieve higher returns. Many retirees don't need retirement income immediately at retirement and elect to defer income from their plans until a later date. This may be a plausible strategy for financial planning today. However, this method may cause disastrous tax liability at death unless proper tools are implemented into your planning.

5. *The use of* **the irrevocable life insurance trust (ILIT)** *is probably one of the most favored tools.* It can be used to replace any applicable tax or combination of taxes. It will allow death proceeds (wealth) to pass without estate tax, income tax, 15 percent excess accumulations tax, generation-skipping tax, state death tax and probate costs. In spousal estates you should consider the use of the joint survivor (second-to-die) life insurance policy to offset the decrease in proceeds due to taxation. The use of life insurance may be optimally

beneficial when a participant plans to defer payment of the 15 percent excess accumulations tax until death. We will discuss this issue further in Chapter 18.

THE 15 PERCENT EXCESS DISTRIBUTION TAX

*T*he 15 percent excess distribution tax "penalizes" all of us for doing a good job of planning for our retirement! ♦

In addition to the 15 percent excess accumulations estate tax, the Tax Reform Act of 1986 (TRA '86) also created a tax for persons who take too much out of their retirement funds. This is referred to as the *15 percent excess distribution tax.* You might have guessed by now that the IRS would obviously reciprocate and find a way to tax those of us who try to reduce our retirement accounts to a nontaxable level to avoid the excess accumulations tax at death.

The IRS now imposes a tax on those who take (in the opinion of the IRS) excess distributions from their retirement plans. The 15 percent excess distribution tax "penalizes" all of us for doing a good job of planning for our retirement! If you have sacrificed, saved and invested well, you will be "penalized." Thus, remember the following two points:

1. *You will be taxed if you take too much* from your qualified retirement accounts when you retire during your lifetime (15 percent excess distribution tax).

2. *You will be taxed if you take too little* from your qualified retirement accounts when you retire during your lifetime and there is a large balance left at your death (15 percent excess accumulations estate tax).

The 15 percent excess distribution tax applies to all excess lifetime distributions after December 31, 1986. The tax is defined and structured in the following two ways according to how distributions are received:

1. Annual distributions (other than lump sum when five- or ten-year forward averaging or capital gains treatment for pre-1974 plan participation is elected) are subject to a 15 percent tax. This tax is applicable to all distributions from all sources received during the year. You will be taxed when the sum of these distributions exceeds the *applicable annual exemption.* Once again the IRS demonstrates how crystal clear it can be when dealing with its largest and best customer—us! The applicable annual exemption is defined as the greater of $150,000 or $112,500. These figures are also indexed

for inflation, utilizing October 1, 1986, as the base period.

2. On lump sum distributions if you elect forward averaging or capital gains treatment, the proceeds will be subject to the 15 percent tax if they exceed five times the applicable annual exemption.

The tax is determined separately for persons receiving lump sum distributions and regular annual distributions.

The 15 percent excess distribution tax is applied to all excess distributions during your lifetime from your qualified plans, including profit-sharing plans, defined contribution and benefit plans. It further includes all ESOPs, 401(a) plans, IRAs, 403(b) plans and 401(k) plans. Benefits received under a qualified domestic relations order are also subject to this tax.

Some planning ideas for the 15 percent excess distribution tax include the following:

- Defer distributions or extend the period over which distributions are taken. Both of these methods allow you to let inflation and tax leverage work in your favor.

- If you have more than one plan, consider combining lump sum distributions with installment payouts. This in effect allows you to double up your exemptions. Excess distribution tax applies separately to lump sum and other annual distributions.

- Reduce contributions to qualified plans and use alternative plans for future contributions.

- Consider taking early withdrawals of IRAs on a lifetime payout basis to eliminate the early withdrawal penalty before age 59½.

Planning for either the 15 percent excess accumulations tax or the 15 percent excess distribution tax is critical. The planning options are complicated and very involved. We recommend that you seek professional help from your estate planner before deciding what action to take.

INCOME TAX ON LUMP SUM DISTRIBUTIONS

In past years we have witnessed that people who receive lump sum distributions from their qualified plans (pension/profit sharing, 401(k), IRA) make the mistake of suffering immediate income tax as well as early withdrawal penalties on the full distributed amounts. This is largely due to the fact they were not aware they could rollover these distributions into their own individual plans and avoid this huge tax liability.

Income averaging provisions were made available to participants who completed five years of participation in the plan and have received a lump sum distribution within one taxable year after reaching age 59½. Those participants who have attained age 50 before January 1, 1986, may use a ten-year forward averaging based on the tax rates that went into effect in 1986. Plan participants must begin taking distributions from their plans on April 1st of the year after they reach age 70½. The amount required to be taken is determined by dividing the plan balance at the beginning of the year by a series of factors laid out in IRS regulations.

The question of withdrawing your funds should be based on the sound financial results attained. If the safety of investment and rate of return is available for the investment fund, whether it is in or out of the retirement plan, and if we assume the rate of return is 8 percent, a major factor will be the income tax ramifications of your decision.

Let's assume that your combined rate for state and federal income tax is 35 percent on lump sum distributions this year and 40 percent for ordinary income for the next ten years. Let's also assume that you are 60 years old, have a plan balance of $800,000 and can either begin to receive payments of income or withdraw the plan balance in a lump sum. You have other annual income of $75,000, and you do not need the income from the plan to support yourself for the next ten years.

If you leave the $800,000 fund in the retirement plan (where it can grow free from state and federal income tax), at the end of the ten-year period of earning (assuming an annual rate of 8 percent), the fund available to produce income will be $1,727,140.

If the $800,000 is taken out in a lump sum today, $280,000 will be lost to income tax, leaving only $520,000 available to produce income. The income produced will be subject to the 40 percent income tax, leaving only a net annual return available to reinvest of 4.8 percent, as opposed to the 8 percent pretax rate.

With reinvestment of all net income, the $520,000 fund will be worth only $831,029 in ten years, as compared to $1,727,140 if the $800,000 fund is left intact in the retirement plan to grow tax-free at its 8 percent rate. Even if the rate of tax this year were much lower than future rates (except in the case of unusual investments), the analyses would show a much better result for financial security by leaving the funds intact in the tax-free retirement plan.

A rule for participants who are married is that financial security for the participant and the surviving spouse is enhanced by leaving the retirement funds intact as long as possible. ♦

In general, a rule for participants who are married (or who soon will be) and who are willing to trust the disposition of the retirement funds to a surviving spouse is that financial security for the participant and the surviving spouse is enhanced by leaving the retirement funds intact as long as possible in a plan where they are undiminished by income tax or estate tax and can continue to grow at a higher rate. This is based on no reduction of earnings each year by future income tax. Putting off withdrawals as long as possible (until age 70½ for most participants) increases the length of time for tax deferral.

The complexity of the tax laws regarding retirement plans is unwieldy at best. Basic questions such as how your plans' benefits will be taxed at your death, how they will pass and how you should utilize distributions during your lifetime should be well thought out and planned for with the help of competent advice. If not, your pension funds may be whittled down to miniscule figures and could result in a tragic loss of hard-earned wealth.

CHAPTER 13

The IRS "Assault" on Your Grandchildren

Extra Tax on Transfers That Skip Generations

*I*f you transfer your assets to your grandchildren, the IRS has a longer period of time to wait before it can tax again. ♦

In addition to federal estate tax at your death, if your estate is large enough and you plan on passing some of your assets directly to your grandchildren, beware!

The IRS has refined their plan to "assault" those of you who wish to skip a generation (your children) and focus your tactical planning on your grandchildren. The same results can occur, even if you plan to divide your estate between both generations—your children and your grandchildren.

This logic is in response to a delayed action of additional taxation to your children. Specifically, if you leave your wealth to your children, it will be taxed again at their deaths under the same guidelines that your estate is taxed at your death. However, if you transfer your assets to your grandchildren, the IRS has a longer period of time to wait before it can tax again. The period is measured by the length of time between the deaths of your children and the extended length of time until the deaths of your grandchildren.

THE GENERATION-SKIPPING TRANSFER TAX (GSTT) OR THE GENERATION-SKIPPING TAX (GST)

Because this tax is a tax on the right to transfer and is applied to direct transfers, it is referred to as the *generation-skipping transfer tax (GSTT)*. This tax is also known as the *generation-skipping tax (GST)*.

In 1976 the first version of the GSTT provided a method of taxation under circumstances when a person had a "power" to control a trust. Applying this concept was the most complex aspect of the original law.

The new GSTT has removed that idea. However, this part of the tax law is extremely complicated and should be approached with great care and expert advice. Complex additions to the law have eliminated this type of planning from do-it-yourself planning techniques.

The new generation-skipping tax can be categorized and summed up as follows:

- The tax is applied based on the relationship of the person receiving property (the **transferee**) and the person who transfers the property or gifts the property (the **transferor**). The tax applies when assets transferred are transferred to or for the benefit of a person or persons at least two generations younger than the transferor, such as the transferor's grandchildren.

- These persons are referred to as **skip persons.** They are at least two generations younger than the transferor. A trust can also qualify as a skip person if the beneficiaries of the trust meet the definition of skip persons.

- Conversely, if a person is a member of the transferor's generation, prior generation or one generation younger than the transferor, this person is referred to as a **nonskip person** (e.g., a transferor's child).

- GSTT is applicable on a transfer or gift to a skip person.

- The GSTT is an additional tax or stand-alone tax. It does not reduce or offset the gift tax or federal estate tax but is in addition to those taxes.

- The GSTT is applied at the maximum unified (gift and estate tax) rate of 55 percent. As with the gift and estate tax structure, which has a $600,000 exemption before any applicable tax is levied, the GSTT also has a *per grantor* exemption of $1 million.

With such a large exemption, many people are under the impression that the GSTT does not apply to their planning. This reasoning, however may not be correct if you implement trusts to protect your children. Planning that provides for property to pass to a trust or trusts for your children at your death, with provisions for income and principal to be paid out to the child (who is a nonskip person), is exempt from application of the GSTT.

WHAT IF YOUR CHILD DIES FIRST?

If you make provisions for the property to go to your child's children (your grandchildren) and the child dies prior to reaching the date of the balance of the distribution of principal, there may be an application of GSTT at that time.

If the trust does not give your child the power that makes the trust includable in his or her estate (such as the power to appoint property to himself or herself, his or her estate, creditors or the creditors of the estate), the death of your child can cause a taxable termination based on the termination of the interest of child (who is a nonskip person) and the transfer of the benefit of the trust to a skip person.

If the child has a general power of appointment or a limited power to appoint property (such as to creditors of his or her estate), then the property will be included in the child's taxable estate and will not be subject to the GSTT. Generation-skipping laws usually apply to most family planning trusts where provisions of gifts to the next generation below the children apply.

The negative aspect of the GSTT is that the property remaining in the trust at a child's death will be subject to tax at the 55 percent rate. Neither the transferor's nor the child's unified credit can be applied against the tax.

If property is distributed outright to the child or if the child has a general power of appointment over the property, it will be subject to estate tax (beginning at the lowest rates) in that child's estate, and the child's unified credit will be applied to tax generated by that property. Since the property is subject to estate tax at the child's level, it will not be subject to the GSTT.

In many circumstances the overall transfer tax may be higher when property is subject to the GSTT as opposed to being includable in the child's estate. If the property is taxed in the child's estate, then the child's unified credit ($600,000 exemption) could shelter up to $600,000 from taxes.

DIRECT GIFTS TO GRANDCHILDREN

Taxing direct gifts to grandchildren requires review of all existing estate plans to determine whether there are any problems created by such gifts. Those who have completed estate planning would be wise to have your plans reviewed to determine whether adjustments need to be considered.

Direct gifts to grandchildren may not be large, but they can become a concern when added together with other property that is not exempt from the GSTT. This property may be kept in trust for your children's lives and thereafter pass to grandchildren. If this is the case, you should consider all the various applications of the GSTT.

A few exceptions to the GSTT that apply to direct transfers to grandchildren are as follows:

- Direct transfers to the transferor's grandchild are, of course, subject to estate tax or gift tax.

- The grandchild's parent is a child of the transferor or a child of the transferor's spouse.

- The parent of the grandchild is deceased at the time the transfer is made to the grandchild.

*D*irect gifts to grandchildren may not be large, but they can become a concern when added together with other property that is not exempt from the GSTT. ♦

If the parent is deceased and we are not skipping the parent in terms of benefit, the rules permit direct gifts to grandchildren that are exempt from the GSTT. The end result is the grandchild moves up a generation. Therefore, that grandchild is considered a child for purposes of application of the GSTT. The trusts that will benefit the grandchild and then go on to benefit that grandchild's children are subject to the GSTT at the grandchild's death to the extent they are not protected by the $1 million per grantor exemption.

TYPES OF GENERATION-SKIPPING TRANSFERS

There are three GSTT applications as follows:

1. **Direct skips.** These are outright transfers. They also include transfers to trusts. These trusts benefit only skip persons.

2. **Taxable distributions.** These are distributions from a trust.

3. **Taxable Terminations.** These are interests in trusts that terminate, such as income rights.

CALCULATING THE GSTT

When you create a trust that is not exempt, or *nonexempt,* the $1 million GSTT exemption is a key part of the calculation of the tax that is levied on a taxable termination, taxable distribution or direct skip.

The complexity of the calculation (ignoring all of the more difficult questions of applying the rules to get to the point of calculation) is beyond the scope of this publication. Estate planners universally agree that because of this complexity, reform in this area of estate taxation needs to occur. It is a law too cumbersome to accurately administer.

Some deductions are allowed, including the amount of certain death taxes, debts, administrative expenses, etc. However, no marital, charitable or casualty loss deductions are allowed as well as no application of the unified credit or $600,000 exemption.

In Chapter 13 we will review additional strategies that offset and enhance the use of the $1 million exclusion. We will also cover the danger of avoiding this tax in smaller estates when doing trust planning that involves the sheltering of the unified credit and qualifying property for the marital deduction in a trust.

PART TWO

Advanced Strategies for Estate Planning

CHAPTER 14

Using Your Deductions

Use Them or Lose Them

THE UNLIMITED MARITAL DEDUCTION

As previously discussed in Chapter 7, legislation introduced by the Reagan administration and subsequently passed allowed property that passes to a surviving spouse to be exempt from estate and gift taxation (ERTA '81). A surviving spouse may be the decedent's second or third (or more!) marriage. This exemption is available to the new spouse on assets transferred to him or her (gifted) or accumulated since 1981.

One exception to this is the 15 percent penalty tax on large accumulations of retirement funds, which was added in 1986 (see Chapter 12). This 15 percent excess accumulations tax is applicable to qualified plans that are top-heavy, overfunded or where minimum distributions are not exercised properly.

THE $600,000 EXEMPTION

The second change made under ERTA '81 was the increase of the unified credit amount to include an exemption through 1986 of $600,000 for *each* individual. This deduction, as well as the unlimited marital deduction, allows estate and gift tax to be deferred and a total amount of $1.2 million to pass from a marital estate tax-free *if planned properly*. Each spouse has a credit that can be applied against estate tax and also has an unlimited marital deduction. Both of these are "use them or lose them" propositions.

When *all* property passes to the surviving spouse—whether by will, contract or right of survivorship (or by intestacy, where a person dies without a will)—the benefit of the unified credit ($600,000 exemption) is lost to the estate of the first spouse to die because there is no tax to be paid at the first spouse's death as a result of exercising the unlimited marital deduction. Because there is no tax to offset, the benefit of the $600,000 exemption is lost forever. This situation in actuality can be referred to as *too much marital deduction.*

All property passes to the surviving spouse, and the entire amount is subject to tax when the surviving spouse dies. The surviving spouse can then use his or her exemption (one $600,000 deduction) only to apply against the tax. The result is that only one credit is used (one $600,000 exemption), and one exemption is lost. The net result of this mistake is the tax savings that the additional exemption is worth (up to $192,800) is unnecessarily charged to the estate. Your heirs lose the potentiality of this inheritance forever.

Another effect of losing the benefit of one unified credit or $600,000 exemption at the first spouse's death is the combination of inflation and growth that may increase the amount subject to tax at the second death. This can produce a disastrous result in terms of increased tax liability. The greater the projected annual growth, combined with the longer projected life expectancy of the surviving spouse, the greater the potential loss if the exemption is not used at the death of the first spouse. If proper planning is used to ensure both exemptions or credits, the potential savings will be great.

*O*ne common misconception in spousal estates is the notion that re-gardless of proper planning, you are entitled to pass $1.2 million estate-tax-free to your heirs. ♦

One common misconception in spousal estates is the notion that, regardless of proper planning, you are entitled to pass $1.2 million estate-tax-free to your heirs. This is a dangerous misunderstanding. Everyone is entitled to the $600,000 exemption. However, unless your estate is arranged correctly with your spouse, one exemption may be entirely lost. In fact, a recent survey of affluent Americans revealed that only 10 percent had previously established the simple estate planning strategies one needs to employ in order to avoid this loss.

How To Avoid Wasting the $600,000 Exemption

To avoid wasting the $600,000 exemption when the first spouse dies, the following two common planning options should be considered.

1. Make arrangements so that at the death of the first spouse $600,000 in property is transferred to individuals other than the surviving spouse. To take advantage of the unified credit or exemption equivalent at the death of the first spouse, $600,000 in property can pass to someone else, such as the decedent's child or children. Providing this person passes exactly $600,000, he or she can take a deduction for this amount and suffer no tax liability.

The balance of assets can then pass to the surviving spouse under the unlimited marital deduction, also without tax liability. This will provide for the use of one exemption at the first death. At the death of the surviving spouse, the remaining exemption can be used, for a total of $1.2 million, passed with no applicable tax liability.

However, sometimes this method may be inappropriate and detrimental to the surviving spouse. Once the equivalent of $600,000 in property passes to individuals other than the surviving spouse, it is no longer available for his or her continued lifetime needs. Caution should be used to ensure that the surviving spouse has adequate additional assets that can be used for income and other purposes for the remainder of his or her lifetime.

As an alternative to removing assets from the reach of a surviving spouse, a second common planning option can be implemented.

2. Pass $600,000 in property to a trust that qualifies for the unified credit and preserves income and other benefits for the surviving spouse's lifetime. A proper plan can provide for an exact amount of up to $600,000 or the exemption equivalent to pass to a trust that usually provides benefits for the surviving spouse. Property put into this trust is subject to estate tax. However, the tax is exactly equal to the unified credit; as a result, there are no taxes due by the surviving spouse or heirs. This type of trust is referred to by several names. The most common names are as follows:

- The unified credit shelter trust
- The bypass trust
- The family trust
- The B trust

Property in this type of trust is treated as not being owned by the surviving spouse for estate tax purposes (if the trust is properly drafted). At the survivor's death, the entire trust passes totally tax-free, including any growth or appreciation in the property.

In addition, the trust income can be used by the surviving spouse and family members. There are limitations on the use of the principal by the surviving spouse, however. The principal can be used for certain standards, such as **health, education, maintenance** and **support,** which are often referred to as **HEMS.**

Such a trust is used to shelter the unified credit of the first spouse to die. Furthermore, the total balance of the trust principal (as well as growth) bypasses estate tax at the death of the surviving spouse, and the total value of the trust can be inherited by other family members.

The balance of the decedent's property in excess of the $600,000 sheltered amount can be arranged to pass to the surviving spouse under the marital deduction, either outright or in a qualifying trust. The balance of property that passes qualifies for the unlimited marital deduction, so no tax is applied on this property. The net tax to be paid (after the benefit of the unified credit) at the first death is zero, regardless of the size of the estate! In Figure 14.1 we show the flow of assets from a marital gross estate to accomplish the use of both spouses' unified credits.

If your combined estate is greater than $12 million, the utilization of this strategy will not avoid estate taxes. It simply defers them. Furthermore, all the marital deduction assets that remain at the surviving spouse's death will be taxed in his or her estate, together with any appreciation or increase in value of those assets. This type of trust arrangement is often referred to as the **optimal marital deduction** plan. You only take a marital deduction on the amount of assets necessary to reduce the net payable tax at the first spouse's death to zero.

*C*haritable gifting has become a premier estate planning tool. ♦

OTHER ESTATE TAX DEDUCTIONS

In addition to the two primary estate tax deductions, the unlimited marital deduction and the use of each individual's unified credit, there are several other estate tax deductions.

Gifts to Charities

Charitable gifting has become a premier estate planning tool. The enormous tax-sheltering effects of charitable giving have produced many estate planning strategies. The tax advantages are generally threefold:

FIGURE 14.1 Flow of Assets from a Marital Gross Estate

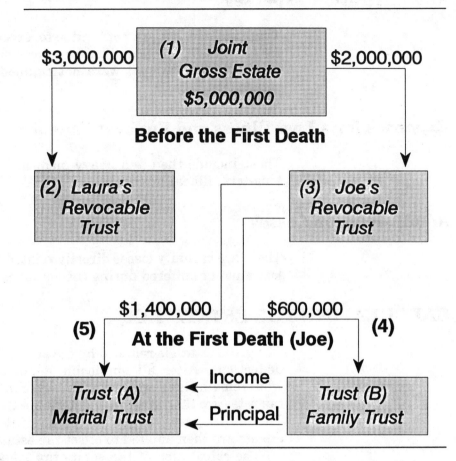

Before the First Death

$3,000,000 — *(1) Joint Gross Estate $5,000,000* — $2,000,000

(2) Laura's Revocable Trust

(3) Joe's Revocable Trust

At the First Death (Joe)

(5) $1,400,000 $600,000   (4)

Trust (A) Marital Trust ← Income ← *Trust (B) Family Trust*

← Principal ←

1. Estate tax avoidance

2. Income tax deductibility for a predetermined remainder interest

3. Capital gains tax avoidance

Because gifts made to charities in trust have become a key planning tool, we will devote more time and considerable explanation to this technique in Chapter 19.

Liabilities of the Decedent

Liabilities include mortgages, unpaid notes, open account balances, unpaid property taxes or other types of assessed or determined taxes or claims that are enforced under state law.

Administration Expenses

These include, but are not limited to, executor's fees, legal fees for court costs, trusts and losses on property during the period of administration that were not claimed on any income tax return, etc.

Expenses for a Last Illness and Funeral Expenses

These include the often heavy medical bills resulting from a long-term illness.

Administration Losses

These are casualty losses directly related to estate assets. The loss must be suffered during the actual estate administration.

CALCULATING THE ESTATE TAX

The gross estate is reduced by the sum total of all the various deductions. After all applicable deductions are subtracted, what remains is referred to as the *net taxable estate*. The estate tax rates are then applied to determine the estate tax payable. The unified credit or exemption equivalent as well as other credits are then applied to offset the estate tax.

The calculation of the estate tax takes into consideration taxable gifts made after 1976. These gifts are valued at their date of gift values. The value of these gifts is added back in and totaled with the net taxable estate. The tax on the total of these two sets of transfers is then calculated. It is at this point that the full amount of the unified credit or $600,000 exemption offsets the tax liability. Any gift tax actually paid on post-1976 gifts is also deducted from the calculated tax. The remaining tax is subject to payment with the estate tax return (Form 706).

The 15 percent penalty estate tax on excess accumulations in retirement plans may apply where amounts held in qualified retirement plans or IRAs are unusually large. This potential income and estate tax trap is discussed in Chapter 12.

ESTATE TAXATION CREDITS

In addition to the various deductions and the unified credit, there are other credits that can be applied to offset estate taxation.

State Death Tax Credit

In Chapter 8 we illustrated the various ways in which states tax estates. Outside of the unified credit or $600,000 exemption, the most important credit is the **state death tax credit,** which is a credit allowed for death taxes that are paid to the states. The maximum amount of credit allowed is reflected on page 52 of Chapter 9.

Foreign Death Tax Credit

To avoid or minimize double taxation on assets owned by those who are subject to taxation in more than one country, the United States has treaties with many foreign countries to provide credits to be applied to the federal estate tax for taxes paid on property in other countries. This is known as the **foreign death tax credit.** These agreements are numerous and extremely complex, and as such we cannot discuss them in detail. It is important to keep this credit in mind when consulting with your estate planner, particularly if you have foreign assets.

Credit for Tax on Prior Transfers

This credit is available when property has been inherited within a certain time frame (usually in the last ten years of life) and is consequently included in a decedent's estate. The amount of the credit usually is based on a percentage of the larger of the tax paid (either in the decedent's estate or in the estate of the person from whom it was inherited). The percentage decreases based on how long ago the property was inherited; recent inheritances receive larger credits. The credit is applicable for the estates of nonresident aliens as well as U.S. residents.

Nonresident Aliens

Estates of nonresident aliens are allowed a credit of $13,000, instead of the $192,800 (the actual tax on an estate of $600,000). Congruently, the $13,000 permitted to nonresident aliens compares to an estate of $60,000. This results in a credit-sheltered estate of only one-tenth the normal exemption afforded to U.S. citizens. This credit is only applicable toward federal estate tax.

The credit usually is greater for citizens of countries with whom the United States has treaties. This currently applies only to Australia, Finland, Greece, Italy, Japan, Norway and Switzerland.

It may be possible for a nonresident alien to avoid both gift tax and estate tax by holding title to U.S. assets in a foreign holding company. The Cayman Islands, Isle of Mann and the Cook Islands are known for having many of these corporations. If these corporations are not treated as shams, the use of a foreign holding company to avoid transfer (estate and gift taxation) taxes on U.S. situated assets has been successful.

Estate tax has been found to apply on assets held by nonresident aliens in U.S. corporations. Gift taxes usually do not apply.

◆ WARNING

This is a very technical area of the law, one that continues to develop. The opportunity for tax sheltering is great. However, a specialist should be consulted whenever this type of planning is being considered.

THE QDOT

Federal estate and gift tax is imposed on taxable estates of all residents of the United States, regardless of where property is located and whether the decedent was a U.S. citizen or a noncitizen. To prevent a noncitizen from removing assets from the United States, the use of the unlimited marital deduction is not allowed. However, the noncitizen surviving spouse can make use of the unlimited marital deduction under the following two provisions:

1. The noncitizen spouse must become a citizen before filing the decedent's federal estate tax return.

2. The property must be passed to a **qualified domestic trust (QDOT)**. No federal estate tax marital deduction will be allowed if the surviving spouse is a noncitizen unless the QDOT is used.

There are specific guidelines that need to be followed when transferring assets to a QDOT. These guidelines go beyond the scope of this book. However, if this applies to your situation, it is important to discuss them with your estate planner and be aware that they need to be followed closely for the trust to qualify for the marital deduction.

In Chapter 15 we will further discuss techniques that allow spousal estates to use both the unified credit and the unlimited marital deduction.

CHAPTER 15

The Magic of Revocable Trusts

A Shelter from the Storm

In Chapter 12 we reviewed the problems presented in spousal estates and the ramifications of not utilizing both spouses' unified credits or the $600,000 equivalent exemptions. The solutions that were briefly mentioned were the bypass trust, B trust, family trust or credit shelter trust. These trusts essentially are all the same.

And in Chapter 6 we outlined the need (especially in estates that contain numerous probate assets) to avoid probate if possible.

In Chapter 3 we discussed the need to plan for the management of your assets in the event of your disability (temporary or permanent) and for the orderly distribution of assets at death.

Trusts can accomplish these tasks and more. In this chapter we will focus on how trusts can be structured to

- plan for your possible temporary or permanent disability;

- avoid probate;

- facilitate the use of both unified credits and in particular the unified credit of the first spouse to die;

- plan for your current spouse or a spouse from a previous marriage;

- omit your current spouse, which may be your second or subsequent marriage, and focus on your own children; or

- make special provisions such as lifetime income to others who are disabled or dependent on you for support for their lifetimes.

TYPES OF TRUSTS

Trusts that are created after an individual dies by a provision in his or her will are called **testamentary trusts.** Trusts that are created during an individual's lifetime and hold title to property are referred to as **inter vivos trusts.** Inter vivos trusts are also commonly called **living trusts, revocable living trusts, loving trusts** and probably some additional titles that we have yet to discover! Regardless of the various titles assigned to the inter vivos trust, these trusts are identical.

*W*ills that create testamentary trusts . . . can be effective estate planning tools. However, wills are ineffective for probate avoidance and disability planning. ♦

Inter vivos is Latin for *living*. We will refer to this trust as a revocable living trust. An additional type of trust, the irrevocable trust, will be discussed in Chapter 17.

The primary difference between the testamentary trust and the living trust is the time at which these trusts are created. As previously stated, the living trust is drafted and executed during an individual's lifetime. The creator is referred to as the *grantor* or *creator.* However, the testamentary trust is created at the death of an individual through a provision in a decedent's will. Testamentary trusts do not hold title to property until the creator or grantor dies. Both testamentary and revocable living trusts can create additional trusts at the death of the grantor that will be covered in detail later in this chapter.

WILLS AS ESTATE PLANNING TOOLS

Wills that create testamentary trusts (family, marital or others) can be effective estate planning tools. However, wills are ineffective for probate avoidance and disability planning, and we do not recommend their use in the majority of estate planning applications as they *contain no living benefits.*

Figure 15.1 illustrates the primary differences between planning with a will and planning with a revocable living trust.

DISADVANTAGES OF WILLS

Some disadvantages of wills are as follows:

FIGURE 15.1 Primary Differences Between Wills and Revocable
Living Trusts

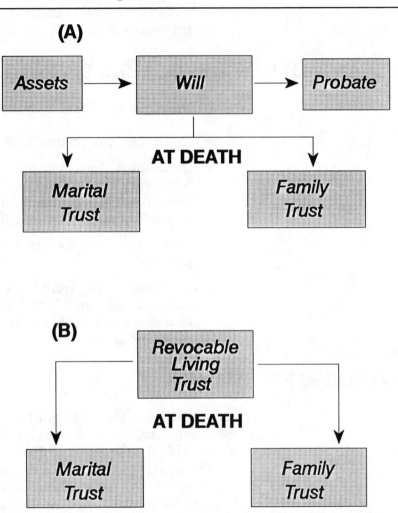

- Your will does not hold title to property and thus contains no systematic provisions for asset distribution to you in the event of your disability. There is no trustee, conservator or guardian. There is no one to step in and manage your assets for you during your lifetime.

- Assets may be titled so that they pass outside the provisions of your will, such as assets held in joint tenancy with right of survivorship (JTWRS) or assets that pass by contract.

- Assets that pass by will are subject to the expense and inconvenience of the probate proceedings.

- Wills can provide for the creation of trusts at the death of the maker. However, quite often these trusts may not be funded properly because assets may pass outside the provisions of the will.

ADVANTAGES OF REVOCABLE LIVING TRUSTS

The advantages of revocable living trusts are as follows:

- Revocable living trusts hold title to assets before death.

- Revocable living trusts provide a center for management when they are funded (i.e., hold title to your property). You can name a trustee, guardian and conservator to act in your behalf during your lifetime.

- Assets held or titled to your trust are not subject to probate.

- Revocable living trusts can split into additional trusts (marital and family), and the grantor can make certain that these additional trusts are funded under the terms of the living trust.

AVOIDING PROBATE

Assets that are placed into a testamentary trust at death *do not* escape probate, such as assets that are titled and owned by an individual at the time of death.

The living trust is created during the life of the grantor and can hold title to assets. When assets are titled to the trust, the trust is "being funded." Assets titled to a living trust escape probate. At death the individual does not own these assets; his or her trust is the actual owner, even though the grantor retains total control of the trust. *If an individual **does not** own an asset at death, the asset will not be subject to probate.*

One of the most common estate planning mistakes we have seen in the last ten years is the neglect of funding, transferring and titling property to living trusts after the trusts are created. Not funding a living trust makes the instrument an absolutely ineffective estate planning tool.

USING THE UNIFIED CREDITS OF BOTH SPOUSES

As we described earlier, a key element in estate planning for spouses is to maximize the use of the unified credits of both spouses. This can avoid a potential federal estate tax of $192,800 in the event that only the surviving spouse's credit is used.

The primary element involved in maximizing the use of the unified credit is to have the first $600,000 of the estate of the first spouse to die pass to a trust. Because this type of trust has several names, we will refer to it as the **family trust** and **trust B** or B trust in the figures in this chapter. Simply stated, it is the trust that holds the $600,000 exemption or shelters the unified credit of the spouse that dies first.

At the death of the first spouse, arrangements can be made for $600,000 in assets to pass to a family trust (trust B). This property, including any increase in its value over time, is sheltered (not taxed) at the death of the survivor, no matter when death occurs! This is true even though the survivor can receive all the income generated by the family trust as well as have access to the principal for the survivor's defined needs.

The attorney drafting the revocable living trust must specifically add language that creates the B or family trust. The exact amount of property going into this trust should not be in excess of the unified credit unless the overall plan intends to create a tax liability at the first death.

In addition, it is absolutely imperative if the estate is large enough that each spouse title at least $600,000 in assets to his or her respective trusts to ensure that at the first death there is at least $600,000 to fund the family trust.

The family trust is usually held for the surviving spouse for the remainder of his or her lifetime. The balance of assets pass to the marital deduction trust. We will refer to this trust as the **marital trust** or **trust A** (also known as A trust).

Figure 15.2 outlines the use of the revocable living trust and the A and B trusts.

The primary element involved in maximizing the use of the unified credit is to have the first $600,000 of the estate of the first spouse to die pass to a trust. ♦

Example

Dan and Kim Young have a combined estate of $1.4 million. They know if arranged correctly they can pass up to $1.2 million without federal estate tax simply by utilizing each of their unified credits or $600,000 exemptions.

They reside in the state of Colorado, a non-community-property state. After talking to their estate planner, they decide to implement the plan outlined in Figure 15.2.

FIGURE 15.2 Sample Plan for the Revocable Living Trust

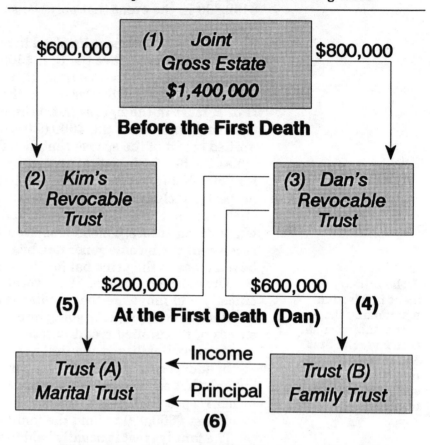

1. They retitle their jointly held assets so that Dan owns $800,000 outright and Kim owns $600,000 outright.
2. Their attorney drafts a revocable living trust for each of them. Dan titles his assets to his trust, and Kim titles her assets to her trust. Both trusts are now funded.
3. Assuming that Dan dies first, his revocable living trust will split out into two separate trusts—A and B. Trust B will be funded with the unified credit amount of $600,000.
4. The balance of Dan's estate will pass to trust A, the marital trust. The $200,000 that is placed into trust A qualifies for the marital deduction.
5. Kim is the trustee of trust A and B and has access to the income and principal from both trusts during her lifetime.

Note: There are other variations of ownership that could achieve the same results. However, for our illustration we assume they each own assets separately.

This simple and easy trust arrangement saved the estate tax on one unified credit or $192,800 in estate taxation.

The Estate Freeze Strategy

In addition to sheltering the $600,000 exemption, a further tax planning tool is created with the family trust. Provided that the surviving spouse has sufficient assets outside of the family trust and has no need to invade the interest or principal of the family trust (trust B) for annual income, this trust may be used as an **estate freeze** strategy. Assets placed in this trust escape estate taxation to the extent of $600,000 at the death of the first spouse. In addition, at the death of the survivor, this trust escapes estate taxation regardless of the total amount of growth.

In the previous example, if we assume the family trust (trust B) holds $600,000 of securities and is able to average 7 percent growth each year and Kim (the surviving spouse) does not withdraw the income or principal, this trust will increase to $1,180,290 at the end of ten years. At Kim's death (the death of the survivor) not only could she use her additional unified credit but the total value of trust B ($1,180,290) can pass to the children with no estate tax. The $600,000 in the family trust in essence was *frozen* and allowed to grow outside either estate and pass tax-free to heirs!

At Kim's death both the A and B trusts terminate and the proceeds pass equally to their two children. Kim's revocable living trust also terminates, and the proceeds of this trust also pass equally to their two children (as illustrated in Figure 15.3).

In this example it is likely that Kim would need the income from the family trust. The balance of assets in the marital trust and her revocable trust may not be sufficient to support her in the lifestyle to which she is accustomed. However, in larger estates the freeze strategy is highly advantageous and readily deployed.

Dealing with Income from the Family Trust

The right to all the income from the family trust may be the easiest formula for dealing with the income, but it may not always be the smartest. This approach will force payments of income to the survivor even in the event they are not needed.

Any income paid to the surviving spouse is taxable as income. Additional income from the trust, together with the survivor's separate property, the marital trust and income that

Any income paid to the surviving spouse is taxable as income. ♦

FIGURE 15.3 Sample Trusts at the Death of the Survivor (Kim)

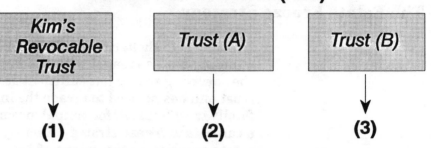

Death of the Survivor (Kim)

| Kim's Revocable Trust | Trust (A) | Trust (B) |

(1)   **(2)**   **(3)**

1. Kim's revocable living trust terminates and is divided equally between her children.
2. The marital trust (trust A) also terminates, and the proceeds are distributed equally to her children. There is no estate tax on the balance of Kim's revocable trust or trust A unless the sum of these trusts exceeds $600,000 (Kim's unified credit). If the sum of these trusts exceeds Kim's $600,000 exemption, her estate will be taxed accordingly. The balance then passes to her two children.
3. Trust B passes tax-free to heirs regardless of the balance of assets contained in this trust.

the survivor continues to receive from employment after the death of the first spouse, may cause additional tax. Income that is not disposed of and allowed to accumulate or compound will be subject to estate tax as a part of the survivor's taxable estate.

If the trustee is allowed to accumulate income in the family trust, this will create an additional taxable entity. Income that accumulates is taxable to the trust and can be divided between the family trust and the surviving spouse. In many cases less income tax will result by not giving all of the income to the surviving spouse.

The Need for a Co-trustee

This type of planning often requires a co-trustee. The co-trustee will be used to distribute income to the surviving spouse. The use of a co-trustee reduces the possibility that the income will be taxed to the survivor even if it is left in the trust.

A danger exists if the trustee has the power to either pay out or accumulate income. If the surviving spouse holds this power as sole trustee, the IRS has taken the position that all of the accumulated income will be taxed to the survivor.

Trust provisions generally provide for a cotrustee to make decisions regarding allocation of income in the family trust.

Tax savings can also be achieved by *requiring* that all income be accumulated in the trust. Through the trustee's powers, arrangements may be made for the trustee to lend accumulated income to herself or himself. This creates a separate income tax entity and the availability of funds to the survivor, with the added benefit of building up a liability (a loan to the survivor) to reduce the survivor's estate for estate tax purposes.

PLANNING FOR YOUR SPOUSE, CHILDREN, LIFETIME INCOME, OTHER FAMILY MEMBERS AND DIVORCE

In many cases estate planning focuses on providing support to minor children for income, education or an array of other objectives. This is a key element in proper planning. If all income from the family trust is required to go to the survivor (as previously mentioned), it will be taxed in addition to other income. The survivor is then forced to use after-tax dollars to pay for such expenses as college or other support for the children.

The Sprinkling Provision

As an alternative, a provision can be structured in your trust so that the trustee can **sprinkle,** or distribute at his or her discretion income among the trust beneficiaries. These beneficiaries can be a group comprised of children, the surviving spouse, parents, an ex-spouse and other people that can benefit from the income. This method may allow a trustee to sprinkle income to others who may be taxed at a lower rate than the surviving spouse. A sprinkling provision can also be an income tax benefit by providing income to children under the age of 14.

Ultimately, a sprinkling provision can be combined with an accumulation provision. This method allows a trustee to pay the income to trust beneficiaries or to let the income accumulate.

Withdrawal of Trust Principal

Another provision of the family trust will allow the surviving spouse to make withdrawals of trust principal within some guidelines.

An income beneficiary usually has a right or the power to withdraw principal from a trust. If the beneficiary fails to withdraw the principal, a gift of the amount not withdrawn is in effect made to the *remainder persons*. These are the people who receive property after the life beneficiary.

A rule exists that allows a beneficiary the right to withdraw the greater of $5,000 or 5 percent of the principal from a trust without causing the entire trust property to be included in his or her estate for federal estate taxation. In addition, the same rule does not trigger gift tax. The $5,000 or 5 percent rule is referred to as the **five and five power** and can give the survivor piece of mind knowing that these withdrawals from the principal can be made.

The five and five power is evident in small trusts, where the survivor may be forced to take principal at various intervals. The amount withdrawn under the five and five power in the year of death will be included in the survivor's estate for estate tax purposes. Withdrawals of principal may be included in the decedent's taxable estate, whereas the principal left in the family trust avoids estate tax at the death of the survivor. It may be advantageous for the survivor to borrow funds if needed from the family trust. A loan will offset any assets withdrawn from the trust. Loans usually result in a net reduction of the survivor's taxable estate in the amount of the unpaid balance.

The family trust is usually held for the surviving spouse and children. If the estate is large enough, the surviving spouse may not have a future need to invade the trust for income or principal. The grantor may arrange for the family trust to benefit others.

A rule exists that allows a beneficiary the right to withdraw the greater of $5,000 or 5 percent of the principal from a trust without causing the entire trust property to be included in his or her estate for federal taxation. ♦

Children from a Prior Marriage

The family trust can be structured to benefit children from a prior marriage. The trust can be formulated to distribute income for a period of time or to a certain age. Ultimately, the trust can distribute the balance of assets outright to the children. This is a widely used family trust provision. In addition, this provision will not disrupt or void the use of the unified credit, as illustrated in Figure 15.4.

As illustrated, the family trust can be divided into a number of different trusts with portions of the property going to or for the benefit of parents, children, grandchildren and children from a prior marriage or marriages. These trusts can favor other people as well as grandchildren. The family trust can be drafted to protect disabled persons that are dependent on income.

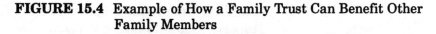

FIGURE 15.4 Example of How a Family Trust Can Benefit Other Family Members

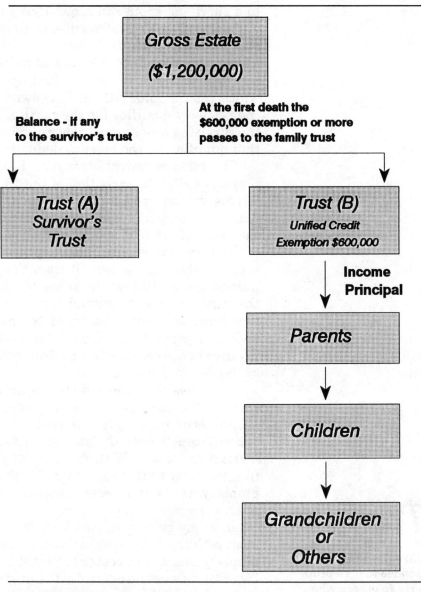

Quite often a grantor may want to give property to individuals that exceeds the amount of the unified credit ($600,000). As such, there will be an estate tax to pay at the death of the first spouse, regardless of other planning. Planning should be done to ensure liquidity for payment of this tax.

THE MARITAL DEDUCTION TRUST (TRUST A)

We have discussed the massive legislation reform created under ERTA '81. These laws had a significant effect on all estate planning. Under the proposals of the Reagan administration, property amounts either given during lifetime or left at death to a surviving spouse in a qualifying manner are subject to a marital deduction that results in no transfer tax (estate tax) applied to the property. Regardless of whether the spouse owns assets valued at $500,000 or $10 million, you can accomplish zero tax at the death of the first spouse. It does not matter which spouse holds title or who owns the property as long as the property qualifies for the marital deduction and is left to the surviving spouse in a proper manner—outright or in a trust that qualifies for the marital deduction.

The marital deduction is now 100 percent of a decedent's property (with the exception of the 15 percent excess accumulations tax on exceptionally large or overfunded retirement plans). All property that qualifies for the marital deduction at the death of the first spouse will be subject to tax at the death of the surviving spouse. This applies only if this person owns it or has the right to benefit from the property. For estate tax purposes, the result is the same whether the property went to the surviving spouse outright, in a qualifying marital deduction trust or always belonged to the survivor. The marital deduction property available for secondary or subsequent beneficiaries of the estate will be offset by the estate taxes payable at the death of the survivor.

Higher estate taxes may be encountered at the death of the survivor if the assets are allowed to grow or appreciate in value.

Assets or property transferred to the surviving spouse without any constraints or "strings" attached are subject to the marital deduction. With few exceptions most property qualifies. Property that does not qualify includes some annuities—property where an interest expires, terminates or is given for a term of years.

In many circumstances transfers made outright may not meet with the donor's objectives. The surviving spouse has the property and the unrestricted right to its use and may abuse his or her power and control of the property. Today a major issue is the right of the surviving spouse to give property to others who are not responsible or who are outside the immediate family circle, such as a new spouse!

A primary concern for each spouse is to whom they would like the property to go at the death of the survivor. And there are no better vehicles than trusts to answer the questions of *who, what* and *when*. Trusts are often used to protect the surviving spouse against himself or herself. This is to ensure that property left for the benefit of the surviving spouse is wisely invested and administered and/or that it is kept intact for the ultimate benefit of the children.

*T*oday a major issue is the right of the surviving spouse to give property to others who are not responsible or who are outside the immediate family circle, such as a new spouse! ♦

Before ERTA '81, property placed in trust for a surviving spouse would not qualify for the marital deduction unless the survivor was given the right of free reign over the property. This power could be delayed until the death of the survivor. The result was that the surviving spouse had the power and control to give the property to anyone, including a new spouse, quite often to the detriment of the donor's children. The largest abuse was usually noted when the children were from a previous marriage.

Under ERTA '81, planning can be revised to eliminate this problem. New laws now allow the marital deduction even though property goes to individuals other than those the survivor would have favored. A spouse can be assured of a marital deduction by leaving property in trust to a surviving spouse and will know that at the spouse's death, the (net of tax) property will pass to the individuals he or she previously designated.

People who have small estates and are exempt from estate taxation may wish to facilitate a trust into their planning notably for the living benefits and also for the protection it affords others, including children they may have interest in benefiting.

SELECTING TRUSTEES

No matter what types of trusts you ultimately select for your estate planning, the selection of a *trustee* or *trustees* is clearly one of the most important steps involved.

When dealing with administration for minor children or for parents and others who may not have the maturity or financial wherewithal to manage and administer funds, a third-party trustee may be the only alternative. Often a bank or trust company will act as trustee.

We encourage clients to choose trustees wisely. Family members are the most widely used individuals. However, in many estate plans, circumstances may not allow you to consider family members. We have found a great reluctance among clients to use outside trustees such as banks.

There is always the possibility that an individual originally chosen to act as trustee will not be able to continue in this role. Trustees can become incompetent, disabled or even predecease the grantor. Comprehensive planning usually provides for a corporate trustee to take over in the event of the death of any individual trustees chosen to act as trustees and secondary or successor trustees.

You can make provisions for the trustee or trustees to elect successor trustees if circumstances dictate. Trusts should contain provisions to facilitate how a trustee should be selected if no appointment is made. This usually is accomplished through petitioning the local probate court and generally requires legal representation that may be expensive and time-consuming.

You may be content using a brother, sister or even a parent for the management of trust assets. These options should be thoroughly reviewed with your estate planner or attorney. However, even if an individual does not have experience in managing money, assets, property, bookkeeping, tax filings and recordkeeping, help is available to assist them to act as trustees.

Visiting with the trust officers at one or more banks or trust companies to explore the possibility of using a corporate trustee is an option worth consideration.

In family situations, quite often one spouse manages the business affairs of the household and even the financial assets during marriage. Consequently, it may be quite normal and fitting to have that spouse step in and serve as trustee if the other spouse predeceases.

*T*he most common arrangement that exists today between spouses is to have each spouse be the trustee of his or her own revocable living trust during his or her lifetime. ♦

The most common arrangement that exists today between spouses is to have each spouse be the trustee of his or her own revocable living trust during his or her lifetime. At the death or disability of the first spouse, the other spouse serves as trustee. We also recommend that individuals consider the use of co-trustees to serve with them in later years.

It is an excellent idea to make provisions to protect and assist in asset management in the event of mental or physical disability. If a surviving spouse has limited experience with asset management or rejects the idea of being put in the position of having to learn to manage assets, a co-trustee arrangement may divert the need for an outside trustee. Often family members can adequately serve as co-trustees.

A co-trustee can provide an array of services to the surviving spousal trustee. Such services can include investment, accounting, tax computation and the day-to-day management necessary for trusts that hold substantial assets and property.

Your trust also should include a provision for the removal of a commercial trustee or co-trustee if needed. The surviving spouse should have the power to seek additional trustees or change trustees in the future. In trusts that provide income to beneficiaries and where beneficiaries have continuing income rights, the beneficiaries should have the right to change trustees. The ability to elect corporate trustees with adequate financial strength should always remain an option.

CHAPTER 16

QTIP and Reverse QTIP Planning

Gaining Control

*P*roperty placed in a QTIP trust flows to people chosen by the grantor or the decedent. ♦

Often trusts will give all rights to income to the survivor for that person's lifetime. At the death of the surviving spouse, the balance of property then passes to a third person. The surviving spouse holds a **terminable interest** in the property because the right to income terminates at the death of the surviving spouse.

Terminable interests usually do not qualify for the marital deduction. There are exceptions to this rule, however. One requirement for qualification under the exception is to make provisions in the trust that prevent the surviving spouse from appointing trust property to herself or himself or to his or her estate.

One such trust that holds property to qualify for the marital deduction is referred to as a **qualified terminable interest property** trust or QTIP trust.

ADVANTAGES OF THE QTIP TRUST

The QTIP trust differs greatly from other types of marital deduction trusts. While provisions under the typical marital trust (trust A) usually allow the surviving spouse to control where the property will go and how it will be used, property placed in a QTIP trust flows to people chosen by the grantor or the decedent. Property in this trust is subject to estate tax at the survivor's death in the same fashion as trusts that give the survivor the power to appoint where property will go.

Control

The function or advantage of a QTIP trust is *control*. The grantor or creator of this trust controls the distribution of property (under the terms of the trust) after death.

In the traditional marital trust (trust A), continued control by the decedent is lost if the trust gives the survivor the right to appoint property distribution or if the property is given outright to the survivor. In the QTIP trust the decedent controls property distribution under the terms set forth by the trust.

The QTIP trust assures a decedent that his or her property will ultimately go to the individuals he or she selects. This trust is widely used to plan for continued income for a surviving spouse. At the death of the surviving spouse, the property can be directed to pass to the decedent's children and not to the survivor's potential new spouse! This planning tool has become a primary strategy in planning for people in second marriages. It is a preventive measure for avoiding the inheritance of property by anyone other than family members. It usually results in a win-win situation for both husband and wife.

Broad Use of the Marital Deduction

QTIP trust arrangements can allow for broad use of the marital deduction. When there are children from a prior marriage involved or children, parents, brothers or sisters who need to be considered in the estate plan, the QTIP trust is a clear winner!

For example, Bill Jones, 63, is a widower who retired two years ago. Bill just married Beth, age 45. Bill has two children from his previous marriage, and Beth has one daughter from a previous marriage. Bill's estate is valued at about $5 million; Beth has a small estate of about $500,000. Because of their age difference, Bill wants to ensure that Beth has adequate income for her lifetime if he predeceases her. Bill also wants to ensure that his assets eventually pass to his children. Bill has not used any of his unified credit and has a revocable living trust in place. Thus, Bill creates the plan outlined in Figure 16.1.

Bill has his revocable living trust updated to create the following three trusts at his death:

1. At Bill's death, his living trust creates a family trust (trust B) to hold his unified credit or $600,000 exemption. Under the terms of the family trust, his spouse has no access to income or principal. All assets in trust B flow to his children in any number of ways that Bill

When there are children from a prior marriage involved or children, parents, brothers or sisters who need to be considered in the estate plan, the QTIP trust is a clear winner! ♦

FIGURE 16.1 QTIP-Family-Marital Trusts

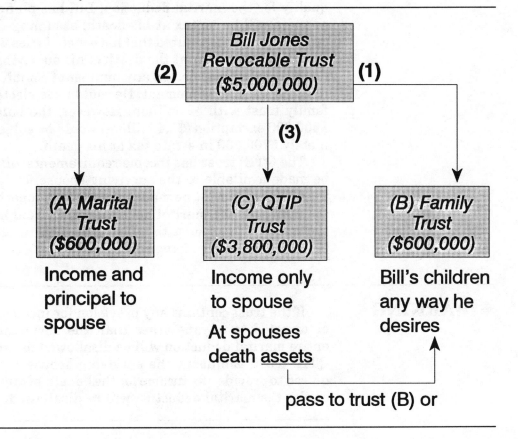

desires. Bill can also amend this trust right up until time of death.

2. Bill also makes provisions in his living trust to create trust A (a marital trust). Bill decides to allocate $600,000 to this trust at his death. This trust will allow his surviving spouse the right to all principal and income in any manner she chooses. She plans to leave this trust for her daughter but may direct its proceeds to anyone.

3. Bill plans to pass the balance of his estate to the QTIP Trust, which is also created at his death by his revocable living trust. Beth will be limited to income only for her lifetime. At Beth's death the QTIP trust will pass to the family trust. The family trust will distribute all trust assets to Bill's children only.

Because Bill elected to fund the B trust (family trust) with no more than his exemption of $600,000, there will be no estate tax due at his death. The balance of his assets will be divided between the marital and the QTIP trusts. Both of these trusts qualify for the marital deduction. Bill has planned his estate so there will be no tax at his death, assuming that he predeceases Beth. He is assured that his beneficiaries will eventually inherit estate assets at the death of his surviving spouse.

Bill could have elected any number of combinations in this multiple trust arrangement. He could have elected to fund the family trust with $2 million. However, the balance over his $600,000 exemption ($1.4 million) would be subject to approximately $700,000 in estate tax at his death.

The QTIP trust has income requirements: *all* income must be made available to the surviving spouse for his or her use. This provision must be made in order for property in the trust to qualify for the marital deduction and avoid being taxed in the estate of the spouse that dies first. This income right must be vested in the *surviving spouse only.*

♦ **WARNING**   If the trust contains any provision for income to be used by or diverted to anyone other than the surviving spouse, the entire marital deduction will be disallowed for property in the QTIP trust. Similarly, the surviving spouse must not be required to provide any income for the benefit of any other person, or else the marital deduction will be disallowed.

THE POWER OF APPOINTMENT TRUST

In addition to the QTIP trust, there is a similar trust that also qualifies for the marital deduction—the **Power of Appointment** trust. A *power of appointment* is a right to direct the trustee to distribute property as determined by the holder of the power. QTIP as well as power of appointment trusts facilitate the ultimate distribution of assets in an estate plan.

Power of appointment trusts have the following two aspects that make them eligible for the marital deduction:

1. The right to all of the income

2. A power to "appoint" the property to anyone. In addition, this includes the following:

   • Uses for the spouse's own benefit.

   • The right to direct the trustee to distribute property as determined by the holder of the power must be present.

- Income payable to the spouse must be received free of constraints.

- No provisions can exist that require the spouse to use income to benefit anyone else.

- The spouse should not be required to do anything that jeopardizes his or her complete and absolute right to all income from the property.

Cases where a seemingly harmless power was vested in the trustee of a trust to deprive the survivor of an income right have disqualified this trust for the marital deduction.

Many attorneys construct limitations on the power of appointment by providing for an effective date of the power to take place after the surviving spouse's death. This does not alleviate the problem of property passing to the survivor's new husband, wife or other family members. Diversion from the surviving spouse of principal that would otherwise provide income to the surviving spouse will trigger the loss of the marital deduction.

It is imperative that powers not be given to anyone (including the spouse) to shift property in the QTIP trust to someone other than the spouse. Use of a QTIP trust will not give the survivor a planning opportunity for reducing estate taxes. Other trusts provide additional planning opportunities to reduce estate taxation by the ability to gift or divert trust assets to others. This may be a drawback of the QTIP trust.

Distributions made to the survivor under the terms of the QTIP trust can be gifted to children or others if the survivor does not need the income. The survivor is free to decide what to do with these funds or assets.

There must be no requirements for the survivor to use the funds in any way. Fund usage must be left strictly to his or her discretion.

QTIP trusts contain a number of drafting issues that can spell disaster in the form of disqualifying the trust for the marital deduction. Small things, such as providing income that is accumulated but unpaid to pass to the next beneficiaries at the surviving spouse's death, may put the marital deduction in jeopardy. Caution should be used, and competent legal advice sought when considering the use of this trust.

FIGURE 16.2 Reverse QTIP Trust

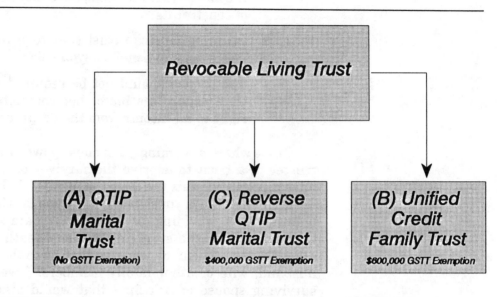

---

*Q*TIP planning
has flexibility that
other marital deduc-
tion arrangements
do not contain. ♦

QTIP planning has flexibility that other marital deduction arrangements do not contain. For example, the QTIP provides postmortem planning based on situations existing at that time, such as the ability to pay some of the tax at the first death (which is an exceptional advantage). An estate that has good growth potential from investing or inflated value assets may minimize estate taxation if some tax is paid early.

Assets that pass to a surviving spouse under the marital deduction generally are treated as being owned by the spouse for the purpose of generation-skipping taxation. If the spouse is the person transferring the property, he or she is referred to as the *transferor* of the property when it passes to the next generation.

THE GSTT AND THE REVERSE QTIP

In Chapter 13 we briefly touched on the generation-skipping transfer tax (GSTT) and how this tax can affect planning techniques. The GSTT has a $1 million exemption. In creating the marital, QTIP and family trust, care should be given so that the exemption is fully utilized. When property in excess of $600,000 (the exemption equivalent) passes under the unlimited marital deduction, the result can cause the utilization of $400,000 of the decedent's $1 million generation-skipping exemption.

The use of the QTIP trust can conserve the decedent's full generation-skipping exemption. This is achieved by providing that the decedent be the transferor of the property in the QTIP trust. This is referred to as a **reverse QTIP,** as illustrated in Figure 16.2.

When generation skipping is an objective in conjunction with the marital deduction, the QTIP trust is a clear winner. Some plans will utilize two QTIP trusts. One will allow the decedent to be transferor, and the other will focus on the spouse as transferor!

SUMMARY

QTIP trusts have three outstanding planning opportunities.

1. Provision of several options for dealing with estate tax at the first death

2. Full use of the marital deduction without loss of control of the ultimate disposition of the assets

3. The ability to preserve the full generation-skipping exemption ($1 million) of the first spouse to die

The unlimited marital deduction and the use of QTIP trust are tantamount in planning for estates of spouses and children, especially if there are children from a prior marriage.

CHAPTER 17

Irrevocable Trusts

The Keys to Disinheriting the IRS

*T*he creator of an irrevocable trust gives up all rights to make any future changes. ♦

Irrevocable trusts are trusts created for the *permanent* transfer of property.

In the previous chapter we discussed the use of the revocable living trust, which people create during their lifetimes to hold title to property until death. The revocable trust may be terminated or amended at any time before the death of the grantor (person that creates the trust). At the death of the grantor the revocable trust becomes irrevocable.

Irrevocable means simply *no changes*. The creator of an irrevocable trust gives up all rights to make any future changes. These trusts usually are set up for the purpose of completing gifts to trust beneficiaries. Gifts to irrevocable trusts are completed gifts with no strings attached. Under the IRS definition, to qualify as a gift, a gift must be irrevocable.

If you transfer assets into an irrevocable trust, you give up complete control of these assets. You cannot revoke or amend the trust. However, you can have some control by drafting the following elements into the trust:

- *Who* benefits from the trust
- *When* they benefit from the trust
- *What* the benefit will be (income, principal, etc.)

The various types of irrevocable trusts are illustrated in Figure 17.1. The three primary uses for irrevocable trusts in estate planning are as follows:

1. Expanding

FIGURE 17.1 Types of Irrevocable Trusts

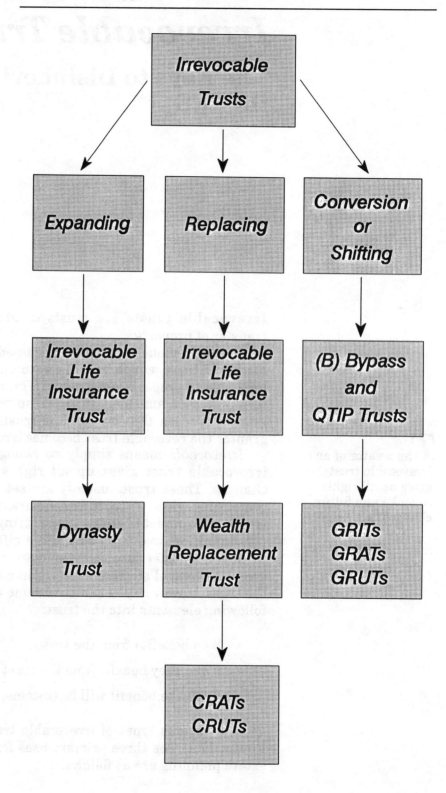

2. Replacing

3. Conversion or shifting

EXPANDING

Expanding trusts are used to create large amounts of cash that remain outside the grantor's estate and therefore are not included in the grantor's estate for federal estate tax computation. The two basic irrevocable trusts used to expand an estate are as follows:

1. The **irrevocable life insurance trust** (ILIT)

2. The **dynasty trust**

Both of these trusts use life insurance to expand an estate. The basic use of the ILIT is to hold enough life insurance to expand the estate to an extent measured by the estate tax liability. The creator typically makes small gifts to children or others that qualify for the annual gift tax exclusion. These gifts are usually waived by donees (persons who receive the gifts) and are used by the trustee of the trust to purchase life insurance. Because the trust is the owner of the insurance, it avoids inclusion in the estate of the grantor. The ILIT can be used to expand a small estate (nontaxable estate) and allow the expanded portion (the life insurance amount) to remain outside the gross estate and not be subject to estate taxation. We will explore the ILIT and its applications in Chapter 18.

The dynasty trust is also an ILIT but is used primarily as a family bank account to provide a combination of income and principal to children, grandchildren and great-grandchildren. This trust usually purchases massive amounts of life insurance. The principal function of the dynasty trust is to avoid the generation-skipping tax by shielding assets inside an irrevocable trust. Application of this trust usually is limited to the ultrawealthy.

Figure 17.2 illustrates the primary use and structure of the ILIT and the dynasty trust.

*T*he ILIT can be used to expand a small estate (nontaxable estate) and allow the expanded portion (the life insurance amount) to remain outside the gross estate and not be subject to estate taxation. ♦

REPLACING

Replacing trusts are used to replace the value of assets due to taxation and settlement costs, and to replace the value of assets gifted to a charity or charities. The irrevocable trusts used to replace assets are as follows:

FIGURE 17.2 The Primary Use and Structure of the Irrevocable Life Insurance Trust and the Dynasty Trust

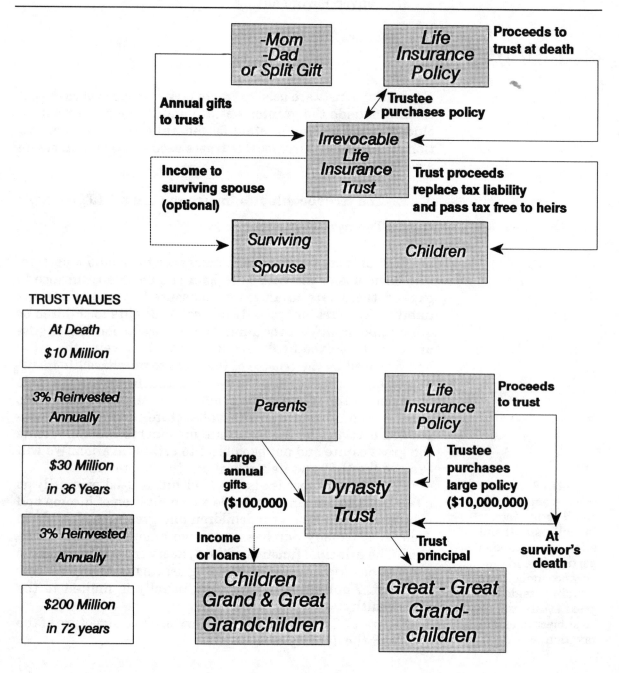

- The ILIT (irrevocable life insurance trust)
- The wealth replacement trust (WRT)
- CRATs (charitable remainder annuity trusts)
- CRUTs (charitable remainder unit trusts)

The ILIT, although used to expand an estate, is more commonly referred to as a *replacing* vehicle because it usually replaces that part of an estate lost to federal estate taxation.

The **wealth replacement trust** is used to directly replace assets given to charity during lifetime or at death. This trust usually is associated with gifts made to charities in trust.

There are several kinds of **charitable remainder trusts (CRTs)** that will be covered in Chapter 19. The two most common CRTs are *charitable remainder annuity trusts (CRATs)* and *charitable remainder unit trusts (CRUTs)*. When a donor makes gifts to a charity in either a CRAT or a CRUT, he or she retains a remainder interest in income from the trust for a certain period or for life. At the death of the grantor the charity retains and owns the gifted asset. Consequently, heirs (such as family members) are deprived of the ability to inherit the gifted assets. Often the donor will elect to replace assets donated to charity with life insurance that will be paid to heirs or other beneficiaries to replace the value of the donated assets. Figure 17.3 illustrates the basic use of the charitable remainder trust.

CONVERSION OR SHIFTING VEHICLES

*I*t is important to remember that provisions are made to create these trusts during your lifetime; however, these trusts are actually created at death and are irrevocable. ♦

In Chapters 15 and 16 we discussed the use of the family trust (trust B) and the QTIP trust (qualifying terminable interest property trust). These trusts are created at time of death either by a provision in a will or a provision in a revocable living trust. It is important to remember that provisions are made to create these trusts during your lifetime; however, these trusts are actually created at death and are irrevocable.

The family trust or trust B, which is also referred to as a bypass trust, is used in spousal estates to qualify the exemption or unified credit of the first spouse to die. As previously discussed, this exemption amount is currently $600,000. Therefore, at the death of the first spouse his or her exemption is shifted to the family or B trust and escapes or "bypasses" estate taxation.

QTIP trusts are used to shift assets away from the surviving spouse. These trusts usually convert assets to income to be paid to the surviving spouse for the remainder of his or her lifetime. They terminate at the death of the surviving spouse and shift

FIGURE 17.3   Basic Use of the Charitable Remainder Trust (CRT)

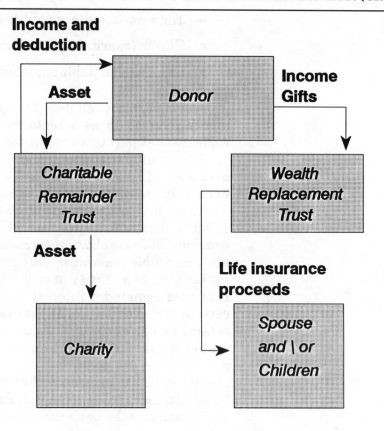

the principal assets of the trust to others whom the grantor has chosen as beneficiaries.

Grantor retained income trusts (GRITs), grantor retained annuity trusts (GRATs) and *grantor retained unit trusts (GRUTs)* are irrevocable trusts that convert assets to income that is paid to the grantor for a period of time. The asset is then shifted out of the estate with an estate tax discount. The use of these trusts will be illustrated in Chapter 20.

SELECTING TRUSTEES FOR IRREVOCABLE TRUSTS

In Chapter 15 we discussed the importance of selecting trustees and the various options available in making this selection. When working with irrevocable trusts, the selection of trustees is critical. In some irrevocable trusts it is imperative that the person creating the trust not act as trustee. Additionally, the use of a spouse as trustee may also cause adverse consequences. One of the potential problems caused by using the person who creates the trust or his or her spouse as trustee is the possibility of having the value of the trust assets at death included in the creator's gross estate. This usually produces adverse tax liability and can negate the original motive for planning and the use of the irrevocable trust. One of the largest uses of irrevocable trusts is to shelter the trust assets from estate tax at the death of the creator.

SUMMARY

Irrevocable trusts are used to expand, replace and convert or shift assets in an estate. Generally, these trusts contain assets that are free of ownership rights by the creation of the trusts. Ultimately, these trusts are estate-tax-exempt and free from all taxation in some cases.

CHAPTER 18

The 1 Percent Solution: The Irrevocable Life Insurance Trust

Taking Revenge on the IRS

In Chapter 17 we explored the different types and uses of irrevocable trusts. In this chapter we will explore in detail the irrevocable life insurance trust (ILIT) and how this basic estate planning tool makes planning for the payment of estate taxes an easy task. The three primary uses of the irrevocable life insurance trust are as follows:

1. To create

2. To replace

3. To expand

CREATING YOUR ESTATE

*T*he availability of cash to pay estate tax liability is tantamount to proper estate planning. ♦

The ILIT can be used to create your estate if you do not have one or if the size of your estate is not sufficient for a surviving spouse or other family members who are dependent upon you for economic support. In fact, this is the classic use of life insurance for the typical American family.

However, there are reasons to create an estate even if your current estate is worth millions of dollars! If your estate is large enough (over $600,000), at death the IRS requires payment of estate tax of up to 55 percent of your entire estate within nine months of death. This single fact may cause the greatest concern to most taxable estates and often is the largest single threat that most estates will face. The availability of cash to pay estate tax liability is tantamount to proper estate planning. Measuring the amount of cash, near-cash equivalent and noncash assets in estate planning is referred to as *estate liquidity*.

Estate Liquidity

Estate assets can be grouped into three separate classifications to determine the degree of vulnerability or direct need for liquidity (cash) at death.

1. *Liquid assets*. These assets include cash or near-cash equivalent assets. Marketable securities, such as stocks and bonds, money market funds and actual cash accounts, are classic examples.

2. *Semiliquid assets*. These are assets that are marketable or convertible to cash but may take a reasonable amount of time to sell or convert. Examples include your personal residence, beach house, ski chalet or other real property that may take up to one year to sell. These assets may be held near and dear by family members or considered to be precious assets by other family members.

3. *Nonliquid assets*. These are assets that cannot be sold or converted to cash or that may take an unreasonable or indefinite amount of time to sell. An example of a nonliquid asset is farmland that may lack a current market. Other examples include closely held businesses, outstanding notes, mortgages and unmarketable securities that have value but no current market for their sale or disposition.

We have found a number of people under the impression that at death, the IRS will collect tax liability from a cross section of all three asset groups. What these people fail to realize is that *you cannot barter with the IRS*. Consequently, the most valuable or precious property may be the first assets converted into cash to pay the IRS tax bill. A family condominium used for family vacations may have to be liquidated well before the farm in Idaho. The estate tax bill is *payable only in cash* and is *due within nine months* of date of death. The IRS collects estate taxes beginning with the liquid (cash) assets of an estate and then requires the estate (or those administering the estate) to convert semiliquid assets and finally nonliquid assets to cash for the balance of the tax liability. Your estate administrators are responsible and required to convert enough assets to cash to pay the tax.

The IRS does not care what problems your estate or those administering it have in converting your assets into cash or what problems are created when all available cash is used to pay the tax liability and heirs are left primarily with nonliquid assets. It does not lament the loss of the earning power of those funds held for the future. The IRS requires that assets be converted to cash now to pay the tax debt, with no sympathy to your estate or heirs.

Figure 18.1 illustrates the true nature of the IRS and the order in which they collect taxes. This order of collecting tax from an estate—or as we say *IRS confiscation*—can cause extreme problems if not properly planned for.

Example

*T*he government has an insatiable cash appetite with no convenient timing to satisfy each individual taxpayer. ♦

Consider the estate of Mr. and Mrs. Charles Johnson. The Johnsons own farmland valued at $3.5 million. The land is currently leased and provides income to Mr. and Mrs. Johnson. Other assets consist of their personal residence, valued at $750,000, and cash of $750,000. Their current estate plan makes use of both unified credits or both spouses' $600,000 exemption. Assuming the death of the survivor occurs in 1994, the estate tax will be approximately $1.7 million. The estate's liquid cash of $750,000 will be confiscated first. This creates a tremendous problem in that the estate is stripped of all liquid assets; all their cash is consumed by taxes and cannot be recovered. If the residence or farmland cannot be sold by the time the tax liability is due, the estate may be forced to borrow funds to complete the tax payment or to sell the properties at liquidation prices. What if assets have to be liquidated in a down market at 50 percent of their normal value? What if the tax bill had been due on October 17, 1987, the day the stock market crashed? *The government has an insatiable cash appetite with no convenient sense of timing to satisfy each individual taxpayer.*

Time is a major factor in regard to liquidating assets. Note here that there is a major obstacle with regard to liquidating real estate for estate tax purposes. Real estate often cannot be sold as fast as needed to facilitate tax payment. Furthermore, in these situations real estate buyers are the only winners. If buyers know your property is for sale under a distressed or

FIGURE 18.1 Order in Which the IRS Collects Taxes

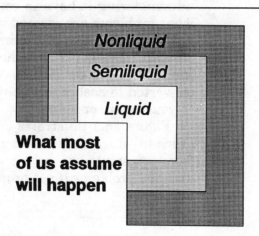

**What most
of us assume
will happen**

Assets

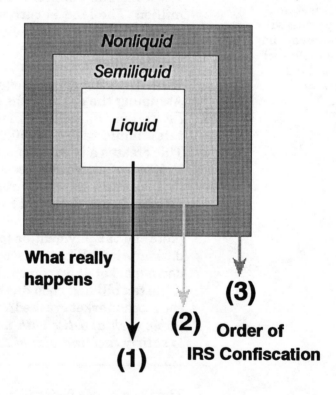

**What really
happens**

(3)

(2)   **Order of**

(1)   **IRS Confiscation**

1. The IRS collects estate tax directly from the liquid assets of an estate.
2. Once all liquid assets are used and a tax balance remains, it requires semiliquid assets to be liquidated.
3. The IRS then looks for nonliquid assets.

forced sale scenario, they are motivated to offer much less than fair market value.

What if property that must be liquidated by heirs is subject to depreciation similar to what was experienced recently in communities such as Denver and Houston, which are oil-industry-based communities? For example, town houses purchased for $100,000 sold for nearly $30,000 during 1990 in Denver.

Estate sales are common in today's economy. We are certain it is not your intent to force heirs to liquidate your assets to pay estate taxes. Liquidation is not the most cost-effective way to deal with tax liability. *We believe liquidation equals federal confiscation.*

If your assets cannot be sold by the time the tax liability is due or your heirs want to retain precious assets, they may be forced to borrow funds to complete the tax payment. In addition to paying back the principal of the loan (the tax bill), they must pay back loan interest. Banks most often charge heirs higher interest rates than they would normally charge you as the money manager. Since you will no longer be involved, your banker will most likely assume your heirs are not as capable as you were to manage the assets.

The IRS will require payment without regard for heirs or others who may be adversely affected by this order of confiscation.

We have witnessed endless examples of problems brought on by the lack of liquidity in taxable estates. The most acute examples usually are those estates that contain business interests. The small family-owned business or closely held corporation is usually the most adversely affected. If cash is deleted from the corporation to pay the estate tax of a primary shareholder, it can strip the corporation or business of operating capital and jeopardize the future operation of the business. Retained earnings paid to stockholders' estates in exchange for stock may be treated as dividend income and trigger adverse income tax liability.

REPLACING YOUR ESTATE

In the last ten years the tax laws affecting estate taxation and so-called "estate freeze techniques" have changed drastically. Tools that were previously effective in keeping your wealth in the family have diminished significantly in plausibility, and in fact many have become obsolete.

In estates that contain sufficient estate liquidity to pay 100 percent of all estate taxation there is still the problem of losing thousands or millions of dollars to federal estate taxation. Wouldn't it be ideal if there were a way in which you could have someone else pay your estate tax bill for you? If someone else satisfied the government's hunger for your wealth, your family could retain not only your cash that is yours to give but all of your other hard-earned assets.

THE 1 PERCENT SOLUTION

There is a way! We call it the **1 percent solution.** Not only is the 1 percent solution the most cost-effective way to pay the tax collector, it's the easiest. It truly is estate planning made easy!

The 1 percent solution allows you to pay your eventual tax bill at 2 to 30 cents on the dollar. It's as if the IRS came to you with the following proposition: "For a limited time, we're going to offer you a way to pay your eventual estate tax bill at a substantial discount. The discount ranges anywhere from 70 to 98 percent, depending on your age. For example, if you pay 10 percent of your current tax liability now, we will guarantee to pay 100 percent of the balance of your estate taxes the day you pass away."

Unfortunately, the IRS doesn't make offers like this. However, the same result can be accomplished for a relatively small monetary commitment (approximately 1 percent or less of your total assets per year) through properly purchased life insurance.

For one reason or another, you may hesitate at the mention of life insurance. Perhaps you have been advised against it by so-called experts in other fields—many who don't fully comprehend the wondrous uses of insurance. Perhaps you're not fully aware of the tremendous leverage and tax advantage it offers. Perhaps you were turned off by an overzealous agent or an uninformed stockbroker. Or maybe you just hate to think of your own mortality.

*T*he bottom line is that the proper type of life insurance, when used correctly, represents a guaranteed investment with an excellent return. ♦

Whatever the reason, put it aside for now. The bottom line is that the proper type of life insurance, when used correctly, represents a guaranteed investment with an excellent return. In some cases the return is as high as 40 to 1! Of course, the actual return will vary based on your age, health, type of coverage and the insurer(s) you select. For a 65-year-old couple, a deposit of $25,000 over seven years can easily produce $1.5 million in tax-free funds to pay estate taxes. This represents an 88 percent discount, or a 20-to-1 return on investment.

To understand the 1 percent solution, it is important to review the tax structure of life insurance death proceeds. Life insurance proceeds *avoid income tax.* If you are the beneficiary of a life insurance policy, you will collect the proceeds *income-tax-free.* If the deceased owned the policy, the life insurance proceeds are included in his or her gross estate for federal estate tax purposes, just as any asset one owns at death.

The problem with personally owning large amounts of life insurance is that not only are the death proceeds fully includable in your gross estate, but these proceeds can push what would have been a nontaxable estate into a heavily taxed estate. If the value of your estate (the sum of assets other than life insurance policies) is under the unified credit amount ($600,000) and you also own an amount of life insurance that when added to the balance of your estate pushes the total over your $600,000 exemption, you will lose a portion of your estate to estate taxation.

Example

Bruce Franz owns a $1 million life insurance policy on his life. He has made his son the beneficiary. Bruce owns additional property valued at $600,000. He dies in a car accident, and his son receives the $1 million life insurance death proceeds income-tax-free. Bruce's estate is valued at $1.6 million for federal estate tax. The estate must pay tax on the value of the insurance proceeds ($1 million) and the balance of Bruce's additional assets ($600,000). The total estate value is $1.6 million for calculating estate tax liability. The federal estate tax due within nine months is approximately $400,000.

If Bruce Franz had no ownership interest in the $1 million insurance policy, he would have no estate tax liability. His estate would have totaled $600,000. His unified credit could be used (assuming he could take a full unified credit deduction) at his death to avoid any tax liability. Bruce could make his son the owner of the policy as well as the beneficiary and thus avoid any inclusion of the death proceeds in his estate. In addition, his son would have no income tax liability when he collects the insurance proceeds at his father's death.

One of the largest uses of irrevocable trusts is to facilitate ownership of life insurance outside the gross estate. The creator of an irrevocable trust can use the trust to apply for and own life insurance policies that prevent insurance proceeds from being included in his or her gross estate.

As an alternative to the irrevocable trust, many people favor naming children as owners and beneficiaries of life insurance policies. The parents are the insured; children or others are the owners and beneficiaries. However, this may cause the following unforeseen problems in the future:

- The life insurance cash values may be subject to your children's or other owners' creditors.

- The life insurance cash values can become subject to spousal election in divorce proceedings.

- Children need to unanimously agree on all aspects of the policy.

- Children or other owners may abuse cash values for their own benefit or avoid paying the premiums even in the event that parents make cash gifts to children with the expectation of premium payment.

- Owners have the right to change the beneficiary designations, and consequently people not included in your plan may ultimately become beneficiaries.

Using the ILIT to own life insurance can eliminate all of these problems and will ensure that life insurance proceeds escape estate taxation at the death of the insured.

In the structure of the 1 percent solution, the ILIT is both applicant and owner of the insurance policy from the onset. This prevents the insured from having any ownership in the policy.

The IRS has strict rules and guidelines concerning the transfer of *existing policies* to an irrevocable trust or other potential owners. If you own insurance policies and you change the ownership (transfer the policies) to other individuals or to an ILIT, you must live for three years before the life insurance proceeds will be excluded from your gross estate. Simply stated, transferring ownership of life insurance that you currently own (to avoid having the death proceeds included in your gross estate) will not exclude it from your gross estate if you die within three years of the date of the transfer. This problem can be avoided with the purchase of new insurance policies if the new policies are applied for and owned correctly at the time of application.

We have found that a large majority of insurance agents who do not work in the estate planning field are unaware of this potential tax trap. Consequently, we have many clients who thought their insurance plans were not included in their gross estates but upon review, discovered the opposite. In fact, we have had clients adamantly state that their insurance agent claimed that their life insurance proceeds would be completely tax-free.

FIGURE 18.2 Ownership and Taxation of Life Insurance
Contracts

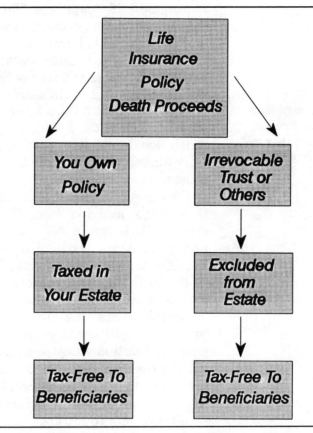

◆ **WARNING**

Life insurance proceeds are received income-tax-free but
are not estate-tax-free if the insured has any incident of ownership. Rights of ownership include the right to change beneficiaries, borrow cash values or exercise any of the standard
nonforfeiture provisions included in the contract. It is vital to
the estate plan that the ownership of life insurance policies
earmarked for estate liquidity be structured correctly. Incorrect ownership will not only cause loss of insurance proceeds
to estate taxation but can significantly increase the estate tax
bracket on the balance of your estate.

Figure 18.2 summarizes ownership and taxation of life
insurance contracts.

The 1 percent solution can be directed to focus on either
estate liquidity needs or complete replacement of estate asset
value lost to estate taxation. In either situation the focus of the

*T*he 1 percent solution can be directed to focus on either estate liquidity needs or complete replacement of estate asset value lost to estate taxation. ♦

plan centers on the use of 1 percent of your estate value. Approximately 1 percent of your estate value is used each year to purchase life insurance. The number of years that premium requirements are necessary varies with your age, health status and the amount of insurance needed to ensure that your estate tax liability is paid or to create sufficient liquidity to avoid all of the problems associated with estates primarily comprised of nonliquid or semiliquid assets.

We refer to it as the 1 percent solution because it is based on 1 percent of the *principal gross estate*. However, it can be much less than 1 percent of your principal estate if partially or fully funded with the growth or income generated from estate assets.

For example, Donald Hayes, a well-to-do businessman from San Diego, and his wife, Charlene, were both age 60 and retired. Their estate was valued at over $4 million. The federal and state estate tax liability was $1,272,600. By earmarking $40,000 per year (1 percent of the $4 million estate) for four years, their tax liability would be covered so that none of their assets would need to be liquidated to pay the tax.

Furthermore, the Hayeses were earning on the average over 10 percent per year on their investments. To create the 1 percent solution, they simply earmarked 1 percent of their income (netting 9 percent) to pay the insurance premium. In other words, for no reduction in principal, using only interest to pay the premium, their future tax liability will be satisfied.

Figure 18.3 illustrates how the 1 percent solution works at various ages and how long premiums are required based on current assumptions. As in the case of Mr. and Mrs. Hayes, for the next four years they will shift $40,000 a year for a total of $160,000 into a tax-free ILIT. In return, their children will receive $1.27 million to pay their estate tax liability.

In Figure 18.3, even though the size of a given estate varies greatly (from $2 million to $10 million), the cost of the insurance remains in proportion to 1 percent of the principal gross estate value. The variable is the number of years/percent the premium will have to be paid based on age and health.

An added feature of the 1 percent solution is that it can make use of your annual gift tax exclusion and have no diminishing effect on your unified credit or $600,000 exemption equivalent! This works extremely well in family situations where you may currently be making small gifts of the annual gift tax exclusion amount ($10,000) or would like to begin making small gifts to children or others and also fund your estate tax liability or solve a liquidity need. Considering the fact that the IRS plans to confiscate up to 55 percent or more depending on total size and types of assets in your estate,

FIGURE 18.3 The 1 Percent Solution at Various Ages

Size of Estate ($)	Approximate Federal and State Tax Liability* ($)	1% Solution Premium / Gift Required ($)	Number of Years To Pay 1 percent** (Joint Equal Age)			
			50	60	70	75
2,000,000	320,000	20,000	1	2	4	6
3,000,000	778,600	30,000	2	3	6	10
4,000,000	1,277,600	40,000	2	4	8	14
6,000,000	2,277,600	60,000	3	5	11	20
8,000,000	3,277,600	80,000	3	5	12	16
10,000,000	4,277,600	100,000	3	5	13	18

*All figures assume the use of both husband's and wife's unified credits or $600,000 exemption. (The total combined exemption equals $1.2 million.) The tax liability for single individuals will be higher.

**The number of years and amount of premium/gift represents the average rates supplied by several companies. The rates are based on standard risks. The length of time for premium payment and the amount of premium/gift may vary according to health history and company interest rates. Our figures assume current rates.

dedicating 1 percent of the principal, or growth, annually for a number of years is drought by comparison. Figure 18.4 illustrates the typical components of the 1 percent solution.

UNDERSTANDING THE 1 PERCENT SOLUTION

The five basic steps involved in the 1 percent solution are as follows:

1. Gifts are made from the gross estate to children or others whom you want to benefit from the distribution of the trust at your death. In the case of spousal estates, the distribution may be made at the death of the surviving spouse. These gifts usually are small (not over $10,000 to each person or $20,000 if both spouses participate in or split the gift) and qualify for the annual gift tax exclusion.

2. The children or others receiving the gifts waive their rights to the gifts. These gifts qualify for annual gift tax exclusion.

3. The trustee then pays the premium for the life insurance owned by the ILIT.

FIGURE 18.4   Typical Components of the 1 Percent Solution

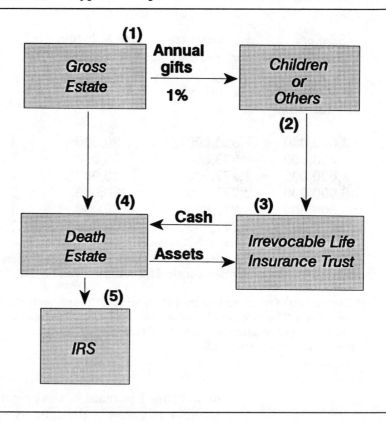

4. The ILIT cannot be directed to pay the estate tax directly. The ILIT can exchange nonliquid assets in the estate for cash so that the estate can pay the estate tax liability.

5. After the tax liability is satisfied, the estate can distribute the balance of assets to heirs or other beneficiaries. The ILIT can terminate and distribute the balance of insurance proceeds (cash) to trust beneficiaries.

There can be several variations on this arrangement depending on what one needs to accomplish and the particular objectives of the estate plan.

In Chapter 14 we explored the use of the family trust (trust B) and the marital trust (trust A) to accomplish the use of both unified credits or both $600,000 exemption equivalents and the unlimited marital deduction in spousal estates. The use of the ILIT in conjunction with these trusts can complete your entire estate planning objectives without any risks or fear of speculative planning strategies.

A review of what this combination accomplishes is illustrated in Figure 18.5.

FIGURE 18.5 Combination of Revocable Living Trust, Marital Trust, Family Trust, QTIP Trust and ILIT

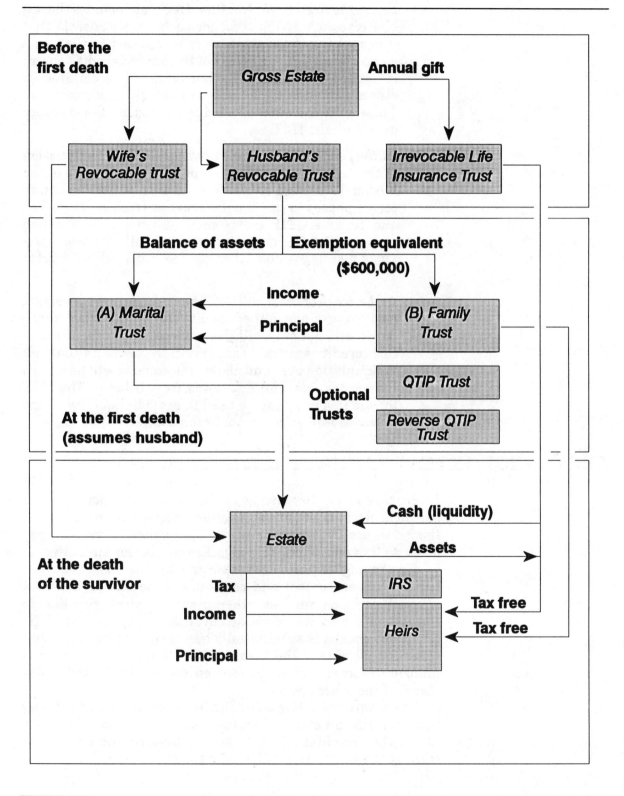

The three phases incorporated in Figure 18.5 are as follows:

- *Before the first death.* Lifetime planning includes the use of a revocable living trust for each spouse. Assets that comprise the gross estate may be retitled so that each spouse owns the equivalent of the unified credit amount ($600,000). Lifetime gifts can be made to children or others that qualify for the annual gift tax exclusion. These gifts can then be used to purchase life insurance owned by the ILIT.

- *At the first death (assumes husband).* The combination of the family trust or B trust provides for the use of the husband's unified credit. The balance of the husband's estate passes to the marital trust or trust A. The QTIP and reverse QTIP trusts may be used to accomplish planning for the surviving spouse, children from previous marriages and other uses as outlined in Chapter 16.

- *At the death of the survivor.* The surviving spouse's estate elects to use her unified credit. The family trust terminates, and not only will the predeceased husband's unified credit amount pass tax-free to heirs but all accumulation over and above this amount will pass both income-tax-free and estate-tax-free to heirs. The ILIT terminates and may be used to provide liquidity to the estate in exchange for nonliquid assets.

EXPANDING OR LEVERAGING YOUR ESTATE

Leveraging refers to shifting to the next generation or other beneficiaries an amount substantially greater than the cost of the insurance. It is a true cost discount by which you can pay a few dollars now to create a significantly larger sum later.

Leveraging is the major reason why life insurance has become a premier tool and continues to be one of the most effective tools as we lose other planning strategies due to changes in legislation. Even at advanced ages, the cost of life insurance usually is substantially less than the face value that would be payable if the insured dies. Even if one spouse is uninsurable, coverage can be secured by using the better health status of the other spouse.

The insurance policy value can leverage or *expand* to many times the amount of the annual premium or gift made to others to pay the premium. Thus, huge transfers can be transacted without the application of transfer taxes.

*L*everaging is the major reason why life insurance has become a premier tool and continues to be one of the most effective tools as we lose other planning strategies due to changes in legislation. ♦

To illustrate this further, John and Mary Westfall recently came to our offices to have us analyze their estate. No previous planning had been recommended. They were burdened with several misconceptions. John, 69, and Mary, 66, were both retired and in good health. After preparing their written estate plan summary (estate analysis), it was determined their net estate value was $11 million. After establishing a revocable living trust with an A/B (marital and family) trust, we estimated their potential estate tax liability at $5 million.

They elected to establish an ILIT and have the trust purchase an equal amount of joint and last survivor insurance. They had considered the alternatives available to pay the $5 million in estate taxes and determined that the 1 percent solution was the most prudent method. Because of their ages and the $5 million needed to insure the estate tax liability, 1 percent, or a deposit of $110,000, is required to fund the trust for a period of seven years. The total deposit of $770,000 over the seven years ultimately represents a return of 7 to 1. This would be almost impossible to create with any other investment because of the income tax and estate tax treatment of the insurance proceeds.

Let's assume that 18 months after the Westfalls adopt the 1 percent solution they die in an auto accident. They completed two years of gifts (premiums). The adoption of the 1 percent solution will facilitate their entire tax liability of $5 million—approximately 22.7 times their original investment. Additionally, they can pass their entire estate intact by simply using 1 percent of their $11 million estate annually!

USING SMALL GIFTS TO FUND AN ILIT

The use of small gifts (to the extent of your annual gift tax exclusion) to fund an ILIT will preserve the unified credit until your death. One of the most advantageous uses of this arrangement is that you give up little control of your estate and estate assets during your lifetime, other than the small annual gifts that you make.

In addition, the insurance trust is extremely easy to administer. Although other assets may be gifted to this trust, it usually contains only life insurance policies. Generally, there are very few management duties that a trustee has to perform. The trustee's main responsibility is to make the premium payments from gifts and collect the death proceeds and distribute these proceeds under the terms of the trust.

USING LARGE GIFTS TO FUND AN ILIT

*I*n late 1992 there was serious consideration given to lowering the amount of the unified credit. ♦

If your estate is large enough and you use proper planning to ensure adequate financial support for the remainder of your lifetime, you may want to consider using your unified credit ($600,000 exemption) and that of your spouse *now* while you are alive!

In late 1992 there was serious consideration given to lowering the amount of the unified credit. Along with their long-term health care bill for the elderly, Representatives Gephardt and Waxman in 1992 proposed a reduction in the unified credit to reflect an exemption of only $200,000. Fearing this change, many people made gifts of their unified credit in hopes of *grandfathering* (the government can never recall the transferred assets) the full $600,000 before proposed reductions could become law. The bill was tabled because of the pending presidential election. However, if you are in a position to gift to the extent of the unified credit amount ($600,000) or in the case of spousal estates the sum of two credits ($1.2 million) during your lifetime, we recommend that you consider doing so before any additional changes in the unified credit are implemented by future legislation.

USING YOUR UNIFIED CREDIT(S) NOW

There are two key elements you should consider when making gifts to the extent of the $600,000 exemption or larger amounts.

1. You should gift appreciating assets if possible.

2. You should leverage your gifts.

Gifting appreciating assets removes the assets from your gross estate and allows them to grow outside of your estate without additional taxation. This is called an *estate freeze*.

The larger your gift, the larger the leverage factor in the ILIT. For example, a 65-year-old couple has an estate valued at $19 million. If both spouses use their unified credits now, they can reduce their estate by $1.2 million. Not only have they reduced the size of their estate, but all potential future growth of the $1.2 millon in assets gifted will be excluded from future taxation. The trust can then purchase insurance up to $10 million with a single premium of $1.2 million to replace death tax liability. In addition, this couple can still make use of their annual gift tax exclusion by making small annual gifts. *Remember, however, no estate tax savings idea should be implemented if it is going to drastically change your lifestyle.*

LAST-SURVIVOR INSURANCE: THE MOST COST-EFFECTIVE WAY TO LEVERAGE YOUR ESTATE

Since the introduction of the unlimited marital deduction under (ERTA '81), which basically transferred the responsibility to pay estate taxes from the surviving spouse to the heirs, a number of insurance companies have introduced a relatively new type of life insurance that's ideal for paying estate taxes. It's called **joint-and-last-survivor** or **second-to-die** insurance.

What makes last-survivor insurance so powerful is its special tax advantages, its tremendous leverage and its low cost. It represents a cost-effective way to preserve your estate for your children and grandchildren.

In essence, last-survivor insurance is designed for married couples. It insures the lives of both spouses under one policy and thus costs less. The proceeds from the policy are used to pay the tax bill when the last-surviving spouse passes away. As such, it allows you to plan your estate so your heirs won't have to liquidate assets or borrow money to pay the tax liability.

If a last-survivor plan is set up properly, the proceeds are paid exactly when they're needed at the death of the survivor. Equally important, these proceeds can be paid to beneficiaries completely income-tax-free, estate-tax-free, probate-free and creditor-free.

Before ERTA '81, the most popular method of providing the necessary funds to pay estate taxes was to purchase life insurance on each spouse. The wife would own the husband's policy and vice versa. Proceeds from each policy were used to pay the tax liability when the time came.

While moderately effective, this method was very costly for two reasons. First, each life had to be insured separately. And second, the vehicles used at that time were expensive whole life policies.

Let's compare the cost of purchasing two separate $500,000 policies on each of two spouses to the cost of purchasing a single $1 million last-survivor plan. (See Figure 18.6.) We assume each spouse is 65 years old and wishes to have the insurance premium vanish in ten years.

As Figure 18.6 illustrates, the last-survivor plan is far less expensive. In our example, it's more than $176,810 less expensive!

After ERTA '81 and the introduction of the unlimited marital deduction, many couples simply insured the youngest spouse. Obviously, they did this because taxes were not due until the surviving spouse passed away.

Insuring only the youngest spouse is, of course, much less costly than insuring both individually. If the younger of the two spouses predeceases the older, the money is put into a trust until it is needed to pay estate taxes. As good as this method may appear, a last-survivor plan is much more economical.

How does a last-survivor coverage compare to insuring the life of only the younger spouse? Even though both spouses are 65 years old, we consider the wife to be younger. That's because insurers, realizing that women traditionally live longer than men, calculate rates for females at four to six years younger than males. If we insure just the wife for $1 million, her ten-year premium total would be $313,860.

However, if we insured both spouses with a competitive last-survivor plan, the total ten-year cost is only $186,980. So insuring both spouses under one last-survivor plan costs approximately 40 percent less in this example than insuring the youngest spouse.

THE DYNASTY TRUST OR FAMILY BANK

As illustrated in Chapter 17, the dynasty trust is an additional application of the ILIT. This trust is often used by the ultrawealthy to accomplish generation-skipping transfers and provide a pool or bank of income for future generations. Figure 18.7 illustrates the use of the dynasty trust.

This type of trust produces income and principal for future generations free of estate and generation-skipping tax. It is often referred to as a *family bank* because income is paid out to children and grandchildren. Children and grandchildren are also allowed to use the trust funds to start businesses, acquire loans, obtain venture capital and start family enterprises.

There are many ways the creator can arrange for income and principal to be paid out to other generations. These trusts are drafted to last for decades, and in some cases more than a century!

LEVERAGING QUALIFIED RETIREMENT PLAN DISTRIBUTIONS TO OFFSET THE MULTITAX ASSAULT

In Chapter 12 we discussed the impacts of income tax, federal estate tax, the additional 15 percent excess accumulations estate tax and the 15 percent excess distribution tax on your qualified retirement plans. The combination of these taxes can confiscate as much as 75 percent of your retirement plans,

FIGURE 18.6 Last-Survivor Plans Can Save You Money

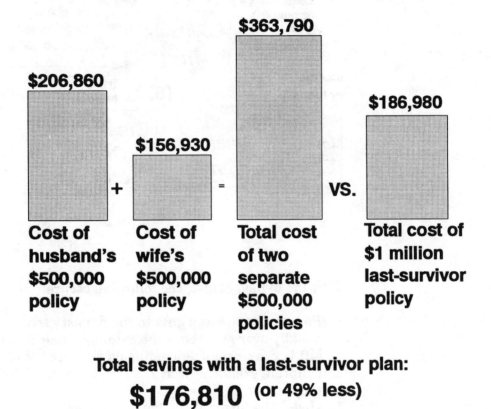

Assumptions: Male, 65, nonsmoker / female, 65, nonsmoker. Need for estate liquidity: $1 million Payment plan: 10 years

$363,790

$206,860

$156,930

$186,980

+

=

VS.

Cost of husband's $500,000 policy

Cost of wife's $500,000 policy

Total cost of two separate $500,000 policies

Total cost of $1 million last-survivor policy

Total savings with a last-survivor plan:

$176,810 (or 49% less)

depending on remaining balances at death and your plan for distribution during your lifetime.

If the balance in your qualified plans places you in jeopardy of paying the 15 percent excess accumulations estate tax, consider taking minimal distributions now! People with large qualified plan balances often defer taking distributions until age 70½. With the advent of working well into our late sixties and early seventies, retirement income may not be necessary. Consequently, many qualified plans become unintentionally *top-heavy* (overfunded).

If this is your situation, consider using minimal distributions now to make small gifts to your children, grandchildren

FIGURE 18.7 The Use of the Dynasty Trust

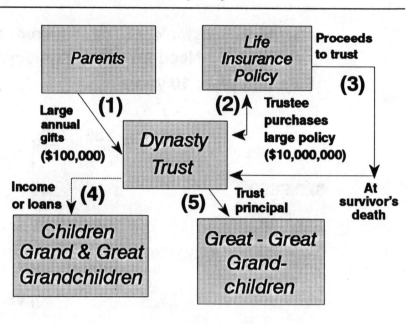

With the dynasty trust, the following occurs:

1. Parents make large gifts to the dynasty trust, usually over and above the extent of their annual gift tax exclusion, depending on the number of children, grandchildren and great-grandchildren they currently have.
2. Under the terms of the trust, the trustee is allowed to purchase large amounts of life insurance. These insurance policies are not limited to but most often are last-survivor life insurance contracts.
3. At the death of the parent or surviving parent the insurance proceeds are paid to the trust.
4. A portion of the trust income can be paid out to children, grandchildren and great-grandchildren. An additional portion of this income is reinvested each year, and the value of the trust multiplies over the course of the lives of the children, grandchildren and great-grandchildren. The fund may have started at $10 million and over the course of 30 to 40 years would be expected to reach $40 to $60 million.
5. The principal portion of the trust is then paid out to great-great-grandchildren.

or others, and allow them to fund an ILIT to replace the inevitable tax liabilities that your estate, including the tax any qualified plans, will incur.

Dr. Sam Stephens recently came to us with a significant estate tax problem and a top-heavy pension plan. Rather than continue accumulating additional interest, we suggested he use a portion of his pension to fund his 1 percent solution program.

In another case, a pension account was surrendered because the client didn't need the income, and the proceeds were used to fund her estate liquidity plan. Never overlook the value and leverage of your pension funds!

USING THE ILIT TO MAXIMIZE THE GENERATION-SKIPPING TRANSFER TAX

Each of us has available under the generation-skipping transfer tax (GSTT) a $1 million exemption for all transfers to skip persons. But if the first spouse to die has less than the equivalent $1 million in assets, some of the potential exemption may be lost. We have also had problems with regard to suggesting that spouses equalize their estate by one spouse gifting assets to another spouse to take advantage of 100 percent of their GSTT exemptions.

The use of a $400,000 insurance policy on the life of the owner of the smaller estate, owned by him or her, often eliminates the complications of one spouse "gifting up" to the other spouse to attain the full $1 million exemption from GSTT. This will facilitate the full use of the GSTT exemption regardless of which spouse dies first or last. However, making full use of the $1 million exemption and accomplishing a zero death tax liability at the death of the first spouse if his or her estate is valued over $1 million is still an issue.

*U*sing the ILIT to provide funds to purchase the stock of a deceased shareholder is a tremendous business planning tool. ♦

Creating more than one QTIP trust is one answer to the dilemma; but this technique becomes complex as the trustee is responsible for additional trust management. And creating two or three QTIP trusts brings a maze of accounting records, tax returns and stress!

Instead, you may elect to have $1,259,600 fund the family trust. The unified credit of $600,000 on this amount and the federal estate tax on the remaining amount ($259,600) leaves $1 million in the family trust to qualify for the $1 million GSTT exemption.

CREATING A MARKET FOR A SHAREHOLDER'S INTEREST

Using the ILIT to provide funds to purchase the stock of a deceased shareholder is a tremendous business planning tool. Having funds available to buy or retain stock upon the death of key persons can directly affect the continuity of closely held businesses. The trust keeps these proceeds out of the estates of other purchasing shareholders. The unique use of the ILIT provides a tax-free purchase or market for the stock.

SUMMARY

For many families, the payment of estate taxes is an ominous obstacle that devours a major portion of their inheritance. The whole affair can be a nightmare; but with proper planning, it doesn't have to be such a disaster.

The 1 percent solution can be designed to

- provide immediate cash at a 70 to 98 percent discount,

- allow your heirs to inherit your estate intact,

- utilize all proceeds received income- and estate-tax-free,

- allow all proceeds to be free from probate and creditors and

- pay your estate taxes at 2 to 30 cents on the dollar.

Figure 18.8 provides a graphic summary of the 1 percent solution.

There is simply no other money management vehicle available anywhere that offers such phenomenal benefits, strong rates of return and superb leverage. The 1 percent solution is the only means to effectively preserve your assets intact for your heirs, protecting the lifetime of hard work and dreams your estate represents.

FIGURE 18.8 Graphic Summary of the Main Benefit of the 1 Percent Solution

Which Check Would You Rather Use To Pay Your Estate Tax?

	3050
A	*TODAY'S DATE* __ 19 __

PAY
TO THE
ORDER OF _ *THE I.R.S.* _____ *$ 1,000,000*

ONE MILLION and 00/100 _____ DOLLARS

MEMO: _____ *ESTATE TAX* _____ _____

YOUR HEIRS

	3050
B	*TODAY'S DATE* __ 19 __

PAY
TO THE
ORDER OF _ *XYZ INSURANCE CO.* _ *$ 10,000*

TEN THOUSAND and 00/100 _____ DOLLARS

MEMO: _ *ONE PERCENT SOLUTION* _____ _____

YOUR SELECTED TRUSTEE

The Choice Is Obvious!

CHAPTER 19

Charitable Giving and the Wealth Replacement Trust
The Only Remaining Tax Shelters

*T*he government is in no position to take on the additional burden of funding charitable institutions nor the vast services they perform. ♦

Charitable giving is rapidly becoming a premier tool in estate and financial planning. Today 90 percent of all charitable gifts come from the private sector. Most likely you are already making contributions to your favorite charity.

The tax laws governing charitable deductions have been in existence for a long time. The only changes to the law have been that current mortality tables and adjustable discount rates are now used in determining the charitable deduction. With an increasing national deficit, it is unlikely that the government will ever disallow the current tax-favored status of charitable giving. Very simply, the government is in no position to take on the additional burden of funding charitable institutions nor the vast services they perform.

WHEN TO CONSIDER CHARITABLE GIVING AS AN ESTATE PLANNING TOOL

If you have any of the following characteristics, you might consider the use of a charitable giving technique even though you might not have a charitable intent.

- You own highly appreciated, low-basis and low-yield property.

- You or your spouse have a top-heavy pension plan. (You cannot make any more deposits.)

- You have a desire to reduce your estate tax liability.

147

- You wish to keep an appreciated asset in the family.

- You want to avoid capital gains tax on the sale of highly appreciated assets.

- You need to shift income or asset value to another family member.

- You want tax-favored income.

- You desire a current income tax deduction.

- You need a cost-effective way to pay estate taxes.

The desire to achieve even one of these objectives will in most cases also provide benefits in one or more of the other areas.

THE USE OF THE WEALTH REPLACEMENT TRUST IN CHARITABLE GIFTING

When assets are gifted to a charity, whether outright or in trust, the charity becomes the ultimate owner of these assets. At death, heirs or other beneficiaries cannot inherit these assets. This is usually why gifts to charity are small and do not include the full value of an estate.

The **wealth replacement trust (WRT)** is an ILIT that holds an amount of life insurance to replace for heirs assets that are gifted to charity. The reasons for making gifts to charity may have nothing to do with your concern for the charity. The enormous tax advantages (income tax, capital gains tax and federal estate tax advantages) gained by the donor are often the primary reason to consider charitable gifting.

CHARITABLE GIFTING TECHNIQUES

The purpose of the following examples and figures is to provide you with a description of each technique; show the cash flows that can be generated; and illustrate how you can reduce your federal estate tax liability, avoid capital gains tax, gain an income tax deduction and increase your income by means of charitable gifting. This is one of the few areas today where everyone wins!

THE CHARITABLE REMAINDER UNITRUST (CRUT)

*T*his is one of the few areas today where everyone wins! ♦

The **charitable remainder unitrust (CRUT)** is designed to pay an annual income to one or more noncharitable beneficiaries for a set period of time or for their lifetimes. At the end of the designated period, the assets in the trust are transferred to one or more charitable organizations specified by the donor.

The amount of income paid to the noncharitable beneficiaries each year is determined by multiplying the value of the trust assets, calculated annually, by a percentage rate that is determined when the trust is created. This percentage must be at least 5 percent and may not be changed. Therefore, the amount of each annual payment to the beneficiaries may vary based on annual fluctuations in the value of the trust and the investment performance of the trustee.

When an individual creates a CRUT, he or she receives a current income tax deduction that is equal to the present value of the future interest ultimately passing to the charity. This tax deduction is subject to certain limitations.

The amount of the charitable deduction is controlled by the following factors:

- The type of charity
- The type of asset or property donated
- The payout rate elected at the creation of the unitrust
- The term of years in which income is to be paid to the beneficiaries and the *annual contribution base* (adjusted gross income) and additional charitable donations

As previously explored, to preserve the *value* of the asset donated to the charity for the heirs of the donor, an insurance policy is purchased to replace all or part of the value of the asset. The premium for the policy can be paid from the donor's newfound income and from the tax savings the unitrust generates. The policy is applied for and purchased by an irrevocable trust to avoid inclusion in the donor's estate. Therefore, the entire value of the life insurance proceeds passes tax-free to heirs. Because the ILIT replaces the donated assets, it is considered to be a wealth replacement trust. Figure 19.1 illustrates the use of a CRUT in combination with a wealth replacement trust.

Another form of charitable remainder trust, the **charitable remainder annuity trust (CRAT),** will be discussed later in this chapter.

FIGURE 19.1 Combination of a Charitable Remainder Unitrust and a Wealth Replacement Trust

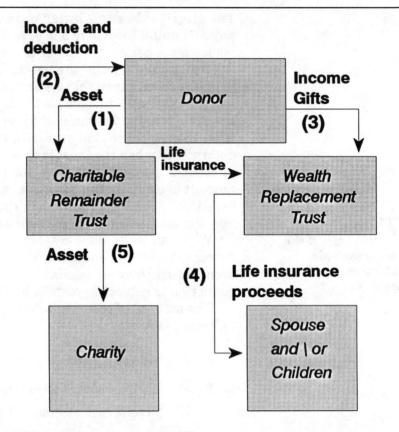

1. The donor transfers asset(s) to the charitable remainder unitrust and avoids capital gains tax on the sale of the asset(s).
2. The donor receives an income tax deduction and income from trust.
3. The donor gifts part of the income to the wealth replacement trust for the purchase of life insurance.
4. When the donor dies, the life insurance replaces the amount that was gifted to the CRUT.
5. At death of the last beneficiary, the ultimate CRUT value is transferred to the charity or charities.

EXAMPLE OF THE CRUT

Sam Peterson is 64 and plans to retire next year. Mary, his wife, is also 64 and is currently involved in charitable work. Mary has not been employed in a professional capacity outside the home. Sam has been employed by and is now a senior executive with a large corporation for the last 25 years. Sam's current salary is $135,000 a year, but his pension with the company will only provide him $50,000 per year before taxes. Sam knows he and his wife will need more than his pension to live on.

With a total estate in excess of $3 million, Sam and Mary are in the 50 percent federal estate tax bracket. Sam and Mary plan to leave a portion of their estate to their church and the remainder to their three children. They are looking for ways to pass as much of their estate as possible without incurring loss through federal estate taxation.

Sam owns a piece of non-income-producing real estate that has a current market value of $1 million. He purchased the land 25 years ago for $100,000. There is no debt associated with the land.

Sam would like to sell the land and reinvest the cash. Sam knows there would be a substantial capital gains tax to be paid (28 percent of the gain). The estimated tax on the sale would be $252,000. This would only leave $748,000 available to reinvest to produce additional retirement income. In addition, the amount he could leave to his children and church will be reduced.

Sam and Mary's goals are to:

- avoid capital gains tax on the sale of the property,

- provide additional retirement income and

- maximize the amount of the estate passing to their heirs and the church.

A CRUT will achieve all the goals Sam and Mary have established.

How the Goals Are Accomplished

Avoid capital gains tax. Sam and Mary establish a CRUT with the help of an estate planning specialist (quarterback) and an estate planning attorney. They then gift the property to the trust. The CRUT sells the land for $1 million. Since the property was sold by the CRUT, there is no capital gains tax to be paid. This creates an immediate savings of $252,000.

Provide additional retirement income. The trust Sam and Mary establish is designed to pay them an annual income for as long as either of them is alive. The trust has $1 million to be invested. They elect that the trust should pay them 8 percent annually. Sam and Mary now have an additional $80,000 per year, before taxes, to supplement their retirement income. If Sam predeceases Mary or Mary predeceases Sam, this stream of income will continue on to the survivor for his or her lifetime.

Maximize the amount of estate passing to beneficiaries. The CRUT will terminate when the survivor dies. At this time the value of the trust ($1 million) will pass directly to their church without tax consequences. Sam and Mary have also used a portion of the annual income and tax savings created by the gift to purchase a $1 million joint survivor policy. The policy is owned by an irrevocable trust with their children as the beneficiaries. The children therefore will receive $1 million totally tax-free to replace the asset given to the charity.

Additional Benefits

By gifting the property, Sam and Mary have removed $1 million from their taxable estate and avoided estate taxes on that amount. In addition, they receive a current income tax deduction for the charitable gift portion of the trust. If they are unable to deduct all of the value of the contribution, they can carry the excess over for up to five years.

Figure 19.2 summarizes Sam and Mary's CRUT, illustrates the benefits the CRUT creates and compares the benefits of the CRUT to the alternative of selling the asset and reinvesting the proceeds. An additional use of the CRUT is to fund for retirement using the tax-favored aspects of the CRUT and the ability to make a large gift to your favorite charity.

EXAMPLE OF THE DEFERRED COMPENSATION NONQUALIFIED ALTERNATIVE

Harold Walters is married and a successful management consultant. He has been in business for himself the past five years. Harold had worked for a firm prior to going into business on his own. He used the pension from his former employment to start his business.

Harold is now 45 years old. Although his income is three times greater now, he is very concerned about his retirement as he used his pension account to start his business. Harold's

FIGURE 19.2 Benefits of the CRUT for Donors Sam and Mary Peterson versus Outright Sale of Property

We have used the following assumptions:

Value of the property donated: $1,000,000

Amount Sam paid for the property: $100,000

Trust rate of return: 8%

Trust payout rate: 8%

Payments to be made: annually

Income tax bracket: 28%

Capital gains tax bracket: 28%

Federal estate tax bracket: 50%

Sam's age on the date of the gift: 64

Mary's age on the date of the gift: 64

	Outright Sale ($)	CRUT ($)	Difference ($)
Asset value	$1,000,000	$1,000,000	$ 0
(–) Capital gains tax	252,000	0	252,000
(+) Tax savings	0	65,520	65,520
(=) Net to invest	748,000	1,065,520	317,520
Average investment income	45,329	63,768	18,529
(×) Number of years	20	20	20
(=) Total net income	904,781	1,275,355	370,547
(–) WRI* premium	0	175,000	175,000
(+) Tax savings	0	65,520	65,520
(=) Net spendable income	904,781	1,165,875	261,094
Asset value in the estate	748,000	0	748,000
(–) Estate tax	374,000	0	374,000
(+) Appreciation	0	0	0
(+) WRI* benefits	0	1,000,000	1,000,000
(=) Net to heirs	374,000	1,000,000	626,000
(+) Future gift to charity	0	1,000,000	1,000,000
(=) Total benefits	$1,278,781	$3,165,875	$1,887,094

*WRI = wealth replacement insurance.

business is incorporated, with ten employees, and he therefore wants to stay away from formal deferred compensation. In actuality, Harold is the business, and now he is interested in exploring the options for retirement income planning.

Harold's current adjusted gross income (AGI) is $150,000, and he is in a 28 percent income tax bracket. His estate tax bracket is 50 percent. He wants to retire at age 65 and can afford to set aside $20,000 per year for his retirement.

Harold's objectives are to

- have the funds grow in a tax-favored environment,

- receive an income tax deduction for the contributions,

- obtain self-completion of the plan in case of premature death and

- leave a gift to the local children's hospital on whose board he sits.

Harold is considering investing in a growth mutual fund. He thinks that such a fund should average 6 percent growth with 3 percent income. At retirement, he would switch to 9 percent Treasury bonds. One problem he recognizes with this approach is the possibility of premature death in that it could leave his family in a financially stressed situation. When he is gone the business will most likely cease to have the value it now has. Then their source of income will end.

How the Goals Are Accomplished

Tax-favored growth.   Harold establishes a CRUT to fund his retirement income. The contributions to the trust may be invested so that there is no tax now on the earnings or growth of the assets.

Income tax deduction for contributions.   Since the contributions of $20,000 per year are to the unitrust, Harold receives a current charitable income tax deduction every year he makes a contribution.

Plan self-completion.   Since Harold wants to be certain that there will be an income stream for his wife if he dies before retirement, the trust purchases and is the beneficiary of a life insurance policy on his life. The premiums are paid from the $20,000 contribution he makes each year to the trust. The annual premium for the policy is $1,600 per year, and the death

FIGURE 19.3 Comparison 1 of CRUT Benefits to Investment Plan for Donors Mr. and Mrs. Harold Walters (Retirement at Age 65)

We have used the following assumptions:
Value of the property donated is ($20,000 × 20 years): $400,000
Trust rate of return: 9%
Trust payout rate: 9%
Payments to be made: annually
Income tax bracket: 28%
Capital gains tax bracket: 28%
Federal estate tax bracket: 50%
Harold's age: 45
Mrs. Walter's age: 45
Harold's age at payout (retirement): 65

	Outright Sale ($)	CRUT ($)	Difference ($)
Asset value	$400,000	$ 400,000	$ 0
(−) Capital gains tax	122,918	0	122,918
(+) Tax savings	0	17,538	17,538
(=) Net to invest	277,082	417,538	140,456
Average investment income	49,343	55,782	6,439
(×) Number of years	20	20	20
(=) Total net income	986,856	1,115,646	128,790
(−) WRI* premium	0	0	0
(+) Tax savings	0	17,538	17,538
(=) Net spendable income	986,586	1,133,184	146,328
Asset value in the estate	874,112	0	874,112
(−) Estate tax	480,761	0	480,761
(+) Appreciation	0	0	0
(+) WRI* benefits	0	0	0
(=) Net to heirs	393,350	0	393,350
Total net income	986,856	1,133,184	146,328
WRI* benefits	0	0	0
(+) Future gift to charity	0	991,028	991,028
(=) Total benefits	$986,856	$2,124,212	$744,005

*WRI = wealth replacement insurance.

FIGURE 19.4   Comparison 2 of CRUT Benefits To Sell and Invest for Donors Mr. and Mrs. Harold Walters (Premature Death)

We have used the following assumptions:

Value of the property donated ($20,000 × 20 years): $220,000

Trust rate of return: 9%

Trust payout rate: 9%

Payments to be made: annually

Income tax bracket: 28%

Capital gains tax bracket: 28%

Federal estate tax bracket: 50%

Harold's age: 45

Mrs. Walter's age: 45

Harold's age at payout (premature death): 56

	Outright Sale ($)	CRUT ($)	Difference ($)
Asset value	$220,000	$220,000	$0
(−) Capital gains tax	104,240	0	104,240
(+) Tax savings	0	11,139	11,139
(=) Net to invest	115,760	231,139	115,379
Average investment income	70,230	114,563	44,333
(×) Number of years	11	11	11
(=) Total net income	702,303	1,145,626	443,323
(−) WRI* premium	0	0	0
(+) Tax savings	0	11,139	11,139
(=) Net spendable income	703,203	1,156,765	454,462
Asset value in the estate	622,068	$0	622,068
(−) Estate tax	342,137	0	342,137
(+) Appreciation	0	0	0
(+) WRI* benefits	0	0	0
(=) Net to heirs	279,930	$0	279,930
Total net income	982,233	1,156,765	174,532
WRI* benefits	0	0	0
(+) Future gift to charity	0	1,015,095	1,015,095
(=) Total benefits	$982,233	$2,171,860	$1,189,627

*WRI = wealth replacement insurance.

benefit is structured to decrease each year as the trust account grows.

Charitable gift to his favorite charity.   The charity will be the beneficiary of the trust assets at the death of the last beneficiary. Since there is insurance in the trust, Harold is assured of leaving a substantial gift to the charity even if he dies prematurely.

Figure 19.3 compares Harold's investment plan to using a charitable remainder trust with a 9 percent payout rate invested in 7 percent tax-free bonds with insurance in the trust. When Harold retires at age 65, the life insurance is surrendered and added to the trust account. Figure 19.4 illustrates the same comparison, but we assume that Harold dies in year 11 of the CRUT. Note that no matter whether he lives or dies, all of his goals are accomplished!

FUNDING FOR ESTATE TAXES USING A CRUT

Another strategic use of the CRUT is for the funding of estate taxes.

Example

Bill Maxwell is 67, and his wife, Linda, is 66. Bill is retired and has an adjusted gross income of $750,000 per year. Their lifestyle is such that they spend almost all of their income. Their estate is valued at $7 million.

Bill and Linda plan to leave their estate to their three children. They also plan to leave a piece of land to the university where Bill and Linda met. This land is worth $1 million and has a cost basis of $200,000. The land is not developed and does not produce an income.

Bill and Linda know that 50 percent of their estate will be eroded by estate taxes. They have put off any planning, but now they are at the age where they realize their own mortality and are willing to discuss their planning options.

Their goals are to

- maintain their current level of spendable income,

- reduce the size of their taxable estate,

- initiate a cost-effective way to pay estate settlement costs and

- make a substantial gift to Bill's alma mater.

These goals will be met by making a deferred gift of the land to the university using a CRUT rather than waiting until their deaths.

How the Goals Are Accomplished

Maintain current level of spendable Income.   They create a CRUT and gift the piece of raw land to the trust. The trust sells the land and pays no capital gains tax. Since the land produced no income and there was no tax to be paid, there has been no effect on their net spendable income.

Reduce the size of their taxable estate.   By gifting the land to the trust, the value of their estate has been reduced by $1 million plus any future appreciation the land may have had. This will result in a corresponding reduction in estate taxes.

Initiate a cost-effective way to pay estate settlement costs.   Having created the CRUT, they have provided a new source of additional cash flow to fund their estate liquidity needs.

The cash flow, which is made up of the tax savings and all the income to Bill and Linda from the trust, is gifted to an irrevocable trust. The trustee uses the gift to purchase a life insurance policy. In most cases the irrevocable trust would be the beneficiary of the life insurance and would use the proceeds to pay the estate taxes.

Make a substantial gift to Bill's alma mater.   The trust assets will pass to the university when both Bill and Linda have died. Should the trustee's investment performance exceed a 9 percent yield, the gift to the university could be well in excess of $1 million.

The objectives in designing the trust are to maximize the cash flow generated and purchase as much last-survivor life insurance coverage as possible. We assume a 9 percent before-tax yield and examine the effects on the cash flow by varying the number of years the trust runs. Our example in Figure 19.5 includes joint lives, 1 life and 17 years certain, and a 10-year

FIGURE 19.5 Comparison of Alternative Trust Periods for Sample CRUT

	Rem. Unitrust	*Rem. Unitrust*	*Rem. Unitrust*
Assumptions	Technique #1	Technique #2	Technique #3
Time period projected	1989–2008	1989–2008	1989–2008
Income payout rate	9%	9%	9%
Income paid	annually	annually	annually
Investment period measured by	2 lives	1 life/17 yrs.	10 yrs.
Contributions			
Fair market value of property	$1,000,000	$1,000,000	$1,000,000
Income tax deduction	247,290	211,350	431,372
Capital gains tax on sale	0	0	0
Cash Flow			
Income during life	1,337,755	1,133,970	741,976
(–) Out-of-pocket premiums	92,530	92,530	92,530
(–) Premiums paid by reinvesting	1,272,955	1,068,492	676,498
(+) Net spendable income	(27,730)	(27,502)	(27,502)
*Estate for Heirs**			
Gross value of estate	0	0	0
(+) Life insurance death benefit	4,740,561	4,266,212	3,750,932
(–) Estate taxes	0	0	0
(=) Net estate for heirs	4,740,561	4,266,212	3,750,932
Benefit Summary			
Net income + net estate			
(=) Total family benefit	4,712,831	4,239,160	3,723,880
(+) Endowment to charity	1,000,000	1,035,352	1,035,352
(=) Total benefit	$5,712,831	$5,274,512	$4,759,232

*Estate for heirs assumes $600,000 exemption not taken.

term. Years certain is the guaranteed number of years the trust would pay out to the creator or other beneficiaries.

EXAMPLE OF MAXIMIZING A CHARITABLE GIFT

John and his wife, Mary, are both 45 years old. They have a joint income of $58,000 per year. Several years ago, one of their children was critically ill. Thanks to the assistance of the local children's hospital, their child has fully recovered and leads a normal life.

John and Mary want to repay the hospital for its help with their child. They decide to begin making cash contributions to the hospital on an annual basis. Their gift currently is $1,800 per year. They would like to do more for the hospital, but their funds are limited.

John wants to make an ultimate gift of $100,000 to the hospital using an insurance policy on his life. He asks the hospital to use his annual gift to pay premiums for the life insurance policy. The hospital is owner and beneficiary of the policy, but John still receives his current deduction for the gift. The policy is designed so that based on current interest assumptions, it will require only ten premium payments.

The after-tax cost of the plan to John will be $12,960 over a ten-year period, and the ultimate gift to the charity will be $100,000.

◆ **WARNING**   Some states will not allow this type of gift because of the insurable interest question. Please check with the charity or an estate planning attorney before making this type of transaction.

ADDITIONAL CHARITABLE GIVING TOOLS

The previous sections have dealt specifically with charitable giving techniques in which life insurance is used as an integral part of the plan to replace the value of the gifted asset. This part of the plan was referred to as the *wealth replacement trust*. In this section, charitable giving techniques are discussed that can but do not necessarily involve the use of life insurance with the wealth replacement trust. *It is important to be familiar with these other concepts as they too are a viable part of the charitable giving and estate planning strategies.*

Grantor Charitable Lead Unitrust

*F*or individuals with large incomes, this provides substantial income tax savings in a current year. ♦

A *grantor charitable lead unitrust* is designed to pay an annual income equal to a fixed percentage of the net fair market value of the trust assets, valued annually, to a qualified charity for a period of years or the lifetime of one or more individuals. At the end of the designated payout period, the assets that had been generating the annual income to the charity revert to a noncharitable beneficiary or beneficiaries.

To determine the amount of income to be paid to the charity, the annual fair market value of the trust assets is multiplied by a fixed percentage. For example, a gift of stock valued on the annual valuation date at $100,000 multiplied by a 5 percent payout rate equals $5,000 paid that year to the qualified charity.

$$\$100,000 \times .05 = \$5,000$$

This form of a charitable lead trust can provide the donor with a large charitable contributions deduction in the year the trust is funded for the ascertaining fair market value of the assets on the date of the transfer into the trust, minus the present value of the remainder interest. However, there is a cost for getting such a large deduction in a given year and designating the noncharitable remainder beneficiaries: the income that is payable to the charity must be included as taxable income (for income tax purposes) by the donor each year. For individuals with large incomes, this provides substantial income tax savings in a current year. The deduction can be used to offset up to 30 percent of the donor's contribution base, with a five-year carryover available for any deduction amount that could not be used in the year of the contribution.

Example of grantor charitable lead trust.   John Lewis has worked for almost 30 years for a computer company. He is a cofounder and major shareholder of the company. Four years ago, the company developed a system for the personal computer market that has Wall Street believing it can be a major player in this arena. Since becoming a public corporation two years ago, his stock has grown from a value of just over $2 million to a recent valuation of $25 million, which represents 40 percent of the outstanding shares or 400,000 shares. The stock pays $4.38 per share in dividends. John and Mary have three grown children and would like to make gifts of some or all of the stock to them and/or their grandchildren, but they want to minimize the gift tax consequences. John's salary from the corporation this year will be about $430,000. After this year (in addition to the income from the stock), John will have a retirement income of $100,000 annually paid from his company's pension plan.

John and his wife are considering retirement at this time. They are looking at ways to plan for their retirement and estate and income tax liabilities. One method is to establish a grantor charitable lead trust in which they would gift $1 million worth of stock to the trust.

By transferring $1 million in stock and providing a 7 percent (equivalent to the current dividend rate) income payout to a qualified charity for John's lifetime (estimated by using a mortality table), they will receive a present value charitable contributions deduction for the value of the income to be received by the charity ($633,414). The remainder of the trust then passes to their children, with a remainder interest value of $366,585.

John's income this year is made up of his $430,000 salary plus stock income of $1,752,000 (400,000 shares × $4.38/share), for a total of $2,182,000. By using this charitable gift arrangement, he receives a substantial deduction against his current adjusted gross income. He can use this to offset up to 30 percent of his contribution base and carry over anything in excess of this amount over the next five years. He can further increase his deduction if he decides to contribute even more shares of stock, but the amount of deduction is still limited to 30 percent of his contribution base in the year of the gift. The "cost" of the large current deduction is that John will be taxed under the grantor trust provisions of the Internal Revenue Code on the trust income as it is earned (as if he had received it).

Figure 19.6 illustrates what John has accomplished by means of this charitable gift arrangement.

Charitable Lead Annuity Trust

A nongrantor **charitable lead annuity trust** is designed to pay an annual income to a charity for a specified period of time, for the life of one or more individuals, or for a combination of the life of a person plus a specified time period. At the end of the agreement, the trust assets are transferred to individuals other than the donor. The trust can be created during a donor's lifetime or by his or her will.

The amount of income paid to the charity each year must be ascertained on the date the property is transferred. It usually is determined by multiplying the fair market value of the property transferred by the annuity rate or may be a stated sum that is fixed at the time the trust is created. The same amount will be paid to the charity each year, regardless of the

FIGURE 19.6 What the Grantor Charitable Lead Trust Can Accomplish

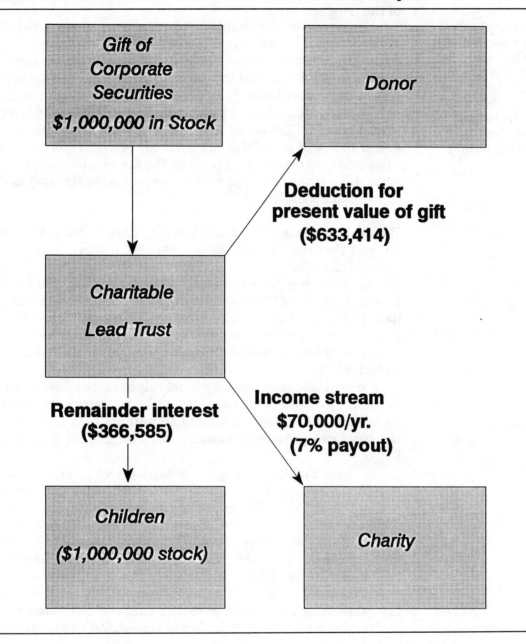

A purpose for creating a nongrantor charitable lead trust is to decrease, for estate or gift tax purposes, the value of the assets that will pass from the trust to the donor's heirs. ◆

fluctuations in the trust value or the investment performance of the trustee.

A nongrantor charitable lead trust does not provide the donor with an income tax charitable deduction. However, income generated by assets within the trust is not taxable as income to the donor, and the donor obtains a gift tax deduction for the present value of future income payable to the charity.

A purpose for creating a nongrantor charitable lead trust is to decrease, for estate or gift tax purposes, the value of the assets that will pass from the trust to the donor's heirs. If the remainder is irrevocably gifted to the donor's heirs, the actuarial value of the remainder on the date of the gift is includable in the donor's estate.

Example of charitable lead annuity trust.   Sam Watts has decided that his church's recent plea for income donations is something he should act upon. He currently owns $1 million of shares in his company's business. The shares were purchased 20 years ago for $150,000. He ultimately wants the shares to pass to his three children but he has no current need for the income generated by them. To help make the church's budgeting process easier, Sam would like to promise a fixed annual donation.

A charitable lead annuity trust might be the best solution for him. By transferring the stock with an appreciated value of $1 million to the trust and using an annuity rate of 7 percent, the trust can provide the church with an annual payment of $70,000.

At the end of the trust agreement, the stock's value will pass to Sam's three children at a decreased value for gift tax purposes of $536,950. (This represents a tax deduction of $463,050, which is the present value of the income interest paid to the charity during the trust years.) If the remainder is irrevocably gifted to the donor's heirs, the actuarial value of the remainder on the date of the gift is includable in the donor's estate.

Sam is able to provide a fixed income to his church during his lifetime and at death pass the value of his stock to his children at a discount. This plan is illustrated in Figure 19.7.

Charitable Gift Annuity

With the *charitable gift annuity,* the donor transfers the asset directly to the charity in return for the charity's agreement to pay a lifetime annuity to the donor. The agreement is backed by the assets of the charity. The charitable contribution is equal to the amount by which the fair market value of the property

FIGURE 19.7   Example of Charitable Lead Annuity Trust

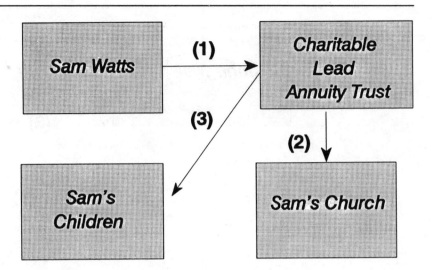

1. Sam transfers $1 million in stock to a charitable lead trust.
2. The trust pays an annual fixed income of $70,000 to Sam's church for his lifetime.
3. At the end of the agreement, assets pass to Sam's children at a discount value for estate and gift tax purposes ($536,950). If the remainder is irrevocably gifted to the donor's heirs, the actuarial value of the remainder is includable in the donor's estate.

transferred to the charity exceeds the present value of the annuity. The steps involved are as follows:

1. The donor transfers the asset to the charity in exchange for a lifetime annuity.

2. Income paid to the donor is secured by the assets of the charity.

3. The donor receives an income tax deduction for a portion of the value of the assets transferred.

Example of charitable gift annuity.   John Wise wants to know the least complicated method for him to donate a piece of property to his local nonprofit hospital. He bought the property 15 years ago for $100,000. Since that time, the property's value has increased to $1 million. He also is interested in receiving income back if at all possible. He does not want to set up a trust.

FIGURE 19.8 Example of Charitable Gift Annuity

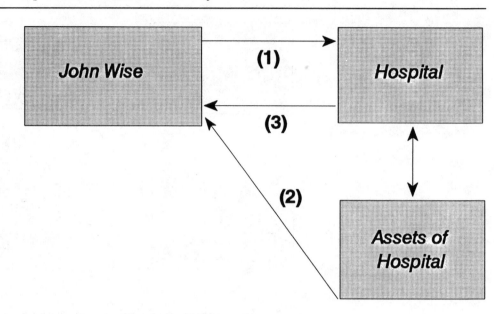

1. John transfers the asset ($1 million) to the hospital in exchange for a lifetime annuity ($1,000,000).
2. The income paid to John ($73,000) is secured by the assets of the charity.
3. John receives an income tax deduction for a portion of the value of the assets transferred ($517,105).

By setting up a charitable gift annuity directly with the hospital, John can accomplish his objectives of simplicity and income. Under this scenario John will give the property to the charity in exchange for a lifetime annuity from the hospital. The hospital will pay John a lifetime annuity of $73,000 annually (based on an annuity factor of 7.3 percent).

John can avoid capital gains tax on the appreciated value of his property and receive an income tax charitable deduction for his gift of $517,105 (the present value of the remainder interest), as illustrated in Figure 19.8.

Charitable Remainder Annuity Trust (CRAT)

A hr *charitable remainder annuity trust (CRAT)* is designed to pay an annual income to one or more noncharitable beneficiaries for a specific amount of time that is no more than 20 years or for the length of the beneficiaries' lives. At the end of the agreement, the assets are transferred to the charity for its use.

The amount of annual income paid to the beneficiaries is determined by multiplying the fair market value of the asset transferred by the annuity rate. This amount is fixed at the time the trust is created but can be no less than 5 percent of the initial net fair market value of the property. The same amount of income will be paid to the beneficiaries each year regardless of fluctuations in the trust value or investment performance of the trustee.

The donor receives an income tax charitable deduction equal to the present value of the future gift that will go to the charity.

Example of charitable remainder annuity trust.   Irma Stricklin, the owner of a chain of dry cleaning stores, is wrestling with the dilemma of what to do with her sizable estate. She has never married. The thought of having a large portion of her estate go to the government for estate taxes makes her cringe. Irma is looking into ways to reduce the taxable size of her estate. She has recently read about the concept of charitable giving and wants to know if there is any way she can give to charity and still retain some of the benefit from her property for herself.

Irma has several pieces of property in her estate that she bought 25 years ago when she was thinking of expanding her dry cleaning empire. One particular piece of property is in a prime development location. She purchased it for only $100,000, and it now has a market value of $1 million.

Irma desires as much certainty in her future as possible. Thus, she considers a CRAT arrangement for her property.

By placing her property in a trust for her favorite charity and having the trust sell the property, Irma can avoid the capital gains tax on the property that she would have paid had she sold it herself. The trust's annuity arrangement will provide her with a fixed annual payment of $70,000 for her lifetime (based on a 7 percent annuity rate).

Irma will also receive an income tax deduction of $536,950 for the present value of her future gift that will go to charity, as illustrated in Figure 19.9.

Pooled Income Fund

With a *pooled income fund,* the assets of one or more donors are transferred to a trust fund maintained by the charity. The fund is designed to pay an annual income to the donors, including their living beneficiaries, for life. At the end of the agreement

FIGURE 19.9 Example of Charitable Remainder Annuity Trust (CRAT)

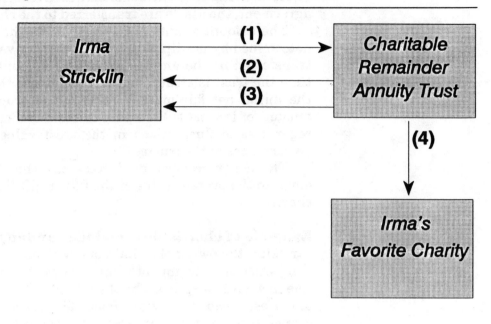

1. Irma gifts the land to a charitable remainder
    annuity trust for her favorite charity.
2. Irma receives an income tax deduction of
    $536,950.
3. Irma receives $70,000 annually for life.
4. At Irma's death, assets in trust pass to her
    favorite charity for its use.

(the death of the last donor), the assets from the fund are
turned over to the charity for its use.

The amount of income paid to the donors each year is
determined by the fund's annual investment performance and
the proportion of the individual donor's contribution.

When an individual makes a contribution to a pooled income fund, an income tax charitable deduction is allowed. It is
equal to the present value at the date of transfer of the future
gift that will go to the charity.

Example of pooled income fund. Some members of the local Congregational church want to create a way for providing
their church with future funding. These people are the charter
members of the church, and they're concerned about what will
happen after they're gone. They themselves are not in financial
positions that would allow them to give large gifts. However,
they feel that if there is a way for them to combine their
resources, their total contribution could be quite substantial.

FIGURE 19.10   Example of a Pooled Income Fund

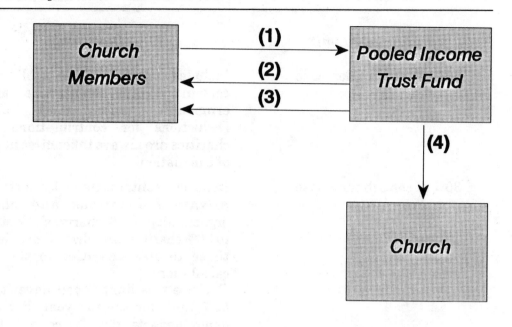

1. Church members gift assets to the pooled income trust fund.
2. Each member receives an income tax deduction for the present value of his or her future gift to the church.
3. Members receive an annual income for life that is based on the unit value of their gift.
4. The remaining value of the trust is passed to the church for its use at the final member's death.

A pooled income fund is the best way to meet their objectives. Under this arrangement each member donates cash or appreciated property to a pooled income trust fund in return for an income tax deduction. They also receive an income for life from the trust based on the value of their gift in proportion to the total trust. After the trust agreement ends at the death of the last donor, the funds are released to the church for its use. Figure 19.10 illustrates the pooled income fund.

The guidelines for establishing various charitable remainder trusts are complex. However, the benefits are outstanding. The summary contained in Figure 19.11 outlines the various points of operation in establishing these trusts. The assistance of a professional is necessary when considering the use of this unique strategy.

FIGURE 19.11 Summary of Income Tax Deduction Rules for Charitable Gifts by Individuals

Annual Limit	*Description*
50% of contribution base	Includes contributions to public charities, certain private foundations and governmental units (50% charities). Deductions for contribu-tions to 50% charities are always taken first in the order of calculation.
30% of contribution base	Includes contributions to certain other private foundations and charitable organizations (30% charities). Contributions to 30% charities are always considered after those to 50% charities in the order of calculation.
	Can use this limit if you haven't used up 50% limit for the tax year. For example, donor deducts 15% for contribution to a 50% charity. Donor can deduct the full 30% for a subsequent contribution to a 30% charity.
Additional limits for capital gains property. (Limits apply when you contribute more than your 20% to your annual contribution base.)	If you contribute certain appreciated capital gains property, your deduction will be subject to 30% and 20% limitations as follows: for contributions to 50% charities, your deduction is limited to 30% of your contribution base; for certain 30% charities, the limit is 20% of your contribution base. There are special rules that limit when these deductions can be made. There also are rules that provide for carryovers.
"For the use of" contributions	Deductions for contributions "for the use of" (rather than "to") 50% charities are limited as follows: the lesser of 30% of the annual contribution base or 50% of the contribution base minus the deductible contribution to 50% charities.
Contribution base	Generally, adjusted gross income for the year in which the contribution is made.

FIGURE 19.11 Continued

Annual Limit	*Description*
Order of calculations for deduction. (You can deduct for contributions until your annual limit is reached.)	First, deduct your 50% charity limit; if your annual limit isn't reached, deduct your 30% capital gains property limit. Next, deduct your 30% charity limit. Finally, deduct your 20% capital gains property limit from your remaining annual limit, if any. For example, assume that you have an adjusted gross income of $60,000. You contribute $5,000 in cash and stock that is worth $20,000 to a 50% charity. You bought the stock two years ago for $5,000. In addition, you give $8,000 in cash to a 30% charity. Your annual 50% contribution limit is $30,000 (50% of $60,000). You deduct your $5,000 cash gift to the 50% charity. Next, you deduct $18,000 of your stock contribution, which is your 30% limit for a contribution of appreciated capital gains property, to a 50% charity (30% of $60,000). The remaining $2,000 for the stock contribution is carried over and can be applied next year to your 30% limit. Finally, you deduct $5,000 of the $8,000 cash gift to the 30% charity and carry over the remainder for use as a 30% limit deduction next year. The reason your 30% charity contribution is limited to $5,000 is that the amount of your remaining 50% contribution limit must be calculated as if you had deducted all of the $20,000 stock contribution instead of only $18,000 ($30,000 less $5,000 cash less $20,000 of stock equals $5,000 unused 50% contribution limit available for your 30% charity contribution).

FIGURE 19.11 Continued

Annual Limit	Description
Carryovers	You can carry over excess contributions for each of the five years after the year of your actual contribution. Carryovers are deducted, with the earliest year first, as follows: after actual gifts made to 50% charities are deducted, then 50% charity carryovers are deducted; if the 50% annual limit isn't used up, actual 30% charity gifts are deducted, and then 30% charity carryovers are deducted.

Amount Deductible	Kind of Property
Full value	Cash or check; long-term stock and most other long-term capital assets.
Donor's basis	Short-term stocks or other short-term assets; inventory and ordinary income property (includes life insurance policies). Long-term capital assets of tangible property if use by the donee is not related to charitable purpose of charity. Long-term assets to certain 30% charities.

CHAPTER 20

Passing the Family Business—SPLITs, GRITs, GRATs, GRUTs, Recapitalization, Buy-Sell Agreements and More Fun!

Avenues under Siege by the IRS

Planning is essential if you want your business to survive after your death. ♦

Today more than ever the laws on business valuation and ownership transfer are highly technical and complex.

Statistics show that *only 30 percent of family-owned businesses survive to a second generation.* In other words, only three out of ten businesses in existence today will pass from one generation to the next. Seven out of ten will go out of business because they failed to design a business continuation plan. Without question, planning is essential if you want your business to survive after your death.

ESTATE FREEZE TECHNIQUES

The *estate freeze* has several meanings with regard to estate planning. It typically involves transferring the growth assets of a family business, such as partnership interests and the common stock of corporations owned by family members, to other family members. The motive, as you might guess, is tax driven. Appreciating assets are transferred from individual(s) in large estate or income tax brackets to individual(s) in lower tax brackets, where these assets escape tax altogether or are taxed at a lower rate. In the case of a true estate freeze, common stock interest, general partnership interests and sole proprietorship interests are converted into debt instruments, preferred stock interests or limited partnership interests.

In the case of federal estate tax, an additional motive is *deferral*. When a senior family member shifts assets to a younger (aged) family member, the death taxes are deferred until the death of the younger family member. A third advantage gained with this type of planning is a built-in generation-skipping transfer, assuming the junior members reciprocate with their planning.

In summary, the estate freeze is a tool that will allow the following advantages within limits:

- The shifting of appreciating assets to avoid and/or lower various tax liabilities

- The deferral of tax liability

- Achievement of a continuity of these benefits to other generations

NO ESTATE FREEZE PROVISION

In 1987 the IRS added what is referred to as the *no estate freeze provision* to the section of law that deals with transfers of property where a retained interest remains. This section of the IRS code is known as Section 2036(c). Sec. 2036(c) underwent changes in 1988 and was redefined by IRS formal notices in 1989 and 1990. It then defined what was includable for federal estate tax purposes for property transferred during the lifetime of an individual.

The rules of Sec. 2036(c) treated people who transferred property during their lifetimes as having a retained life estate in the property. This rule applied specifically to those who transferred an interest in property having substantially disproportionate rights to the appreciation while retaining any interests in the enterprise.

An example of this is the recapitalization of common preferred stock. A parent or senior family member transfers appreciating common stock to junior family members or children and then retains preferred stock. Under Sec. 2036(c), the common stock would be included in the grantor's (parent's) estate and is subject to taxation.

The rules of Sec. 2036(c) applied entirely to family members and the transfer of business wealth from senior family members to junior members. This section of the code was at best difficult to interpret. The uncertainty forced many businesspeople as well as advisers to use methods that were specifically approved under Sec. 2036(c).

The most widely used transfers during this period were as follows:

- *Buy-sell agreements.* Used formulas based on fair market value at death.

- *Grantor retained income trusts* (GRITs). The grantor retained an income for the period of ten years.

- *Transfers of business interests.* These were proportionate with respect to appreciation and income rights.

- *Irrevocable life insurance trusts* (ILITs). Had no retained rights.

In 1990 Sec. 2036(c) was repealed retroactively and replaced with Sections 2701–2704. Under these new laws Congress seeks to prevent family members from transferring business wealth to other family members (largely parents to children and grandchildren) to avoid estate and gift taxes. The main focus of these areas of law is valuation of the business and manipulation of value.

*T*he freeze will result in gift and estate tax savings only if certain rights are retained by the transferor that have *value.* ♦

These new laws essentially address *valuation* as it applies to gift tax laws on transfer of assets to family members (junior members) of the enterprise. It is very clear that the IRS will now look at senior family members as transferring the entire property value gifted to junior family members for gift tax purposes. The exception is when the senior family member retains certain rights!

The freeze will result in a gift and estate tax savings only if certain rights are retained by the transferor that have *value.* A+ tax liability will apply if these rights are later altered or limited.

DETERMINING THE GIFT

When determining the value of a gift for gift tax application of the *controlled* business interest (corporation or partnership) by the transferor and transferred outright or in trust to a member of the transferor's family, the transferor retained interest is deemed to be $0.

In the eyes of the IRS, this eliminates overvaluing or phoney or disguised gifts. Congress provided an additional safety factor when the transferor or family member retained rights to qualified payments on preferred stock. If the payments are not made at the time or in the amounts used in valuing these rights, the transferor's taxable gifts may be significantly increased to reflect values based on the actual distributions made. These valuation rules apply to a transferor who has a controlled interest in the transferred corporation or partnership.

- A *controlled corporation* is a corporation represented by 50 percent of the stock owned by the transferor.

- A *controlled partnership* is a partnership represented by 50 percent of the capital and profits owned by the transferor.

TRANSFERS IN TRUST

Before the Revenue Reconciliation Act of 1990, a family member could establish and gift assets to an irrevocable trust and retain an income interest for a term of years. This is similar to the charitable remainder unitrust and the charitable remainder annuity trust. These trusts, however, were between a donor and a family member, not a donor and a charity. At the end of the specified term of the trust, the trust principal and any appreciation could pass to beneficiaries such as children or grandchildren. These trusts presented the opportunity to transfer assets with substantial appreciation potential at a gift tax value that was much less than their actual value with the potential appreciation added in.

With the passage of the Revenue Reconciliation Act of 1990, these trusts' interests no longer qualified and were eliminated.

The following are the two primary trusts that effectively were eliminated:

1. *The grantor retained income trust (GRIT).* This is an irrevocable trust into which a grantor places assets and retains an income interest for a term of years. At the end of the term, the principal in the trust plus the full appreciation passes to the trust beneficiary, usually children or grandchildren of the grantor.

2. *The split purchase (SPLIT).* A SPLIT is a purchase of property by one family member that is then treated as a transfer of a term or remainder interest to another family member. The price paid for the property does not include any account of possible appreciation. Thus, appreciation can effectively be passed on to another family member without effecting an increased gift tax for appreciation. SPLITs are still a viable tool that can be used outside of a family transaction.

The provision in the Revenue Reconciliation Act of 1990 that eliminated the effectiveness of transferring appreciation at gift tax value left a loophole. A retained *qualified interest* in a trust by a transferor (applicable family member) is now valued higher. This reduces the value of the future interest gift to the trust or remaindermen beneficiaries and reduces the gift tax cost.

QUALIFIED INTERESTS

Qualified interests are defined as follows:

1. *Fixed amounts.* Payable at least annually (such as a fixed annuity interest that closely resembles a charitable remainder annuity trust interest).

2. *Fixed percentages.* Amounts payable at least annually that are a fixed percentage of the trust's asset value that is determined annually (such as a variable annuity that closely resembles a charitable remainder unitrust interest).

3. Any noncontingent remainder interest if all other interests in the trust qualify under numbers 1 or 2 above.

GRATs and GRUTs are defined as follows:

- *GRAT.* The grantor retained annuity trust interest. This is the right to receive *fixed amounts* annually.

- *GRUT.* The grantor retained unitrust interest. This is the right to receive *fixed percentages* of the trust assets annually.

Tax-Saving Results of GRATs and GRUTs

Figure 20.1 illustrates the estate tax savings of a senior family member who transfers income-producing assets to a junior family member.

Potential Problems with GRATs and GRUTs

In Figure 20.1 the savings in estate tax are great. However, there are some potential problems.

If the grantor with the retained interest term (ten years in Figure 20.1) survives the term of the GRAT, the securities, including any appreciation after the transfer, will be excluded from his or her gross estate. If the grantor dies prior to the expiry of the ten-year term, it will create a retained life interest (Sec. 2036(c)). The entire full date of death value will then be included in the grantor's (senior family member's) estate. This

FIGURE 20.1   Example of Tax Savings by Establishing a GRAT

Value of securities transferred	$1,000,000
Term of the trust	10 years
Grantor's age (senior family member)	62
Valuation rate	10%
Year-end annuity payout	$100,000
Value of retained income interest	$614,556
Value of remainder interest (taxable gift)	$385,544
Growth rate of securities (assumed)	5%
Value of securities at ten-year termination	$1,628,895
Amount passing free of transfer tax	$1,243,351
Estate tax savings (50% applicable rate)	$621,676

*T*he most scruti-
nized aspect of buy-
sell agreements
under the new laws
is valuation of
closely held busi-
nesses. ♦

holds true for both the GRAT and GRUT. In other words, these trusts will be nullified.

An additional danger is the possibility that the grantor will not survive the terms of the trusts; and as such, the trust property will not pass to the spouse, and therefore no marital deduction can be used.

The grantor also loses control of the transferred assets, and only the remainder persons will receive the assets at his or her death. There may be other heirs the grantor would like to focus on at death. Additional estate liquidity may be necessary depending on the total estate tax liability and the type of additional assets held by the estate.

Solutions to the GRAT and GRUT Problems

The wealth replacement trust (irrevocable life insurance trust) can be used effectively to deal with these problems.

Note the following solutions:

- If the term of the trust is ten years, the grantor can use the wealth replacement trust to offset the tax liability in the event he or she predeceases the term of years and is therefore faced with additional tax liability.

- Life insurance in the wealth replacement trust can be used to replace assets passing to remainder persons and allow the grantor to leave cash or assets to additional heirs. The wealth replacement trust also can be used to equalize gifts among other family members who are not included in the GRAT or GRUT as beneficiaries.

In the previous example in Figure 20.1, in which the family member transfers securities valued at $1 million to a GRAT, the amount passing tax-free to the beneficiary is calculated at $1,243,351. Assuming the grantor does not live for the full (i.e., ten-year) term of the trust, he or she could replace the potential tax savings ($621,676) in an irrevocable life insurance trust (ILIT). The amount passing to the beneficiary ($1,243,351) could also be duplicated in an ILIT and used to equalize the amount of gifts to other children or trust beneficiaries.

RECAPITALIZATION OF CORPORATIONS AND PARTNERSHIPS

The recapitalization freeze permits the transferor to shift wealth to the next-level generation (senior family member to junior family member) by the reduction of gift tax. However, to be effective, requirements under the new laws (i.e., Sec. 2701) must be met.

The following transfers qualify for Sec. 2701 and should be considered tools to reduce your tax base:

- *Same type transfers.* The senior family member transfers common stock to junior members and retains common stock.

- *Proportional transfers.* The senior family members transfer proportionate amounts for common and preferred stock to junior family members.

- *Qualified payments.* These involve the transfer of common stock where the common stock is at least 10 percent of the value of the corporation or greater and the senior family member retains preferred stock. The preferred stock should have a cumulative declared fixed dividend.

BUY-SELL AGREEMENTS

Buy-sell agreements are formal agreements (contracts) between the business entity and shareholders or owners that spell out what will happen (if anything) when a shareholder or owner becomes disabled, wants to sell his or her interest, wants to retire or dies. Will the business buy his or her interest if he or she wants to sell, or will other shareholders buy the interest?

Who will control the business at the death of an owner or shareholder?

The most scrutinized aspect of buy-sell agreements under the new laws is valuation of closely held businesses. The new laws do not favor fixed valuation. Losing the ability in agreements to arrive at a fixed dollar value gave a clear understanding of what problems lie ahead. Planning for proper liquidity and applicable death taxes was systematic.

Buy-sell agreements created after the tax law changes must focus on two tests:

1. *There must be a specific business purpose for the agreement.* In the eyes of the IRS, this test will prevent these agreements from passing business interest to family members at a much discounted or bargain price. Stricter evidence of value may invoke the use of outside (costly) appraisals done on a frequent basis to meet this test.

2. *The buy-sell arrangement must be compared to other such agreements.* This test is thought (again by the IRS) to be a "prove all" of validity for an agreement. Would you have entered into the same agreement with a third party? Is this deal too good to be a bona fide agreement? Factors to contend with in meeting this test are as follows:

   • The term of the agreement

   • A close look at the present value of the property

   • Value at the time the agreement is exercised

   • Consideration for the agreement

These elements need to be strategically incorporated into any new buy-sell agreement. They are technical and should be implemented only with professional help.

CHAPTER 21

IRS Tax Relief
Not Really

Under normal circumstances the federal estate tax must be paid within nine months of death. For business owners, when the value of their estates includes illiquid business interests, the IRS will allow deferred payments of estate taxes if certain strict regulations are followed.

SECTION 6166: DEFERRED TAX PAYMENTS

*F*or business owners, when the value of their estates includes illiquid business interests, the IRS will allow deferred payments of estate taxes if certain strict regulations are followed. ♦

Section 6166 of the IRS code makes provisions for deferred tax payments. The availability of this provision depends on whether the gross estate holds a business interest that exceeds 35 percent of the total adjusted gross estate. If an individual owns several businesses in his or her estate, they may be combined as long as he or she owns 20 percent of each concern.

The amount that your estate may defer is the amount attributed to your qualified interest in the business. The installments may be deferred for five years and nine months from the date of your death. The tax payments can be made over a total maximum period of 14 years. This is from the period due date, nine months after date of death and a four-year initial deferral period, followed by up to ten annual payments. During the four-year deferral period, your estate must pay interest at a fixed rate. On the first million of liability, the rate is 4 percent. However, this is reduced by the unified credit exemption. The balance then varies according to IRS published rates.

This section of tax deferral applies to all types of businesses from sole proprietorships to corporations.

SECTION 303 REDEMPTIONS: CORPORATE STOCK

This section of the IRS code pertains to corporate stock redemptions only. Section 303 qualifies what would ordinarily be considered dividend income and turns it into nontaxable income!

When corporations redeem stock, distributions to shareholders usually are treated as dividends. The exceptions to this are as follows:

- The shareholder's entire interest must be redeemed.

- The redemption must be substantially disproportionate.

- The redemption must not be the equivalent of a dividend.

Sec. 303 permits a partial redemption to qualify as a sale when the following guidelines are accomplished:

- The redeemed stock must be included in the decedent's gross estate.

- The value of the stock must exceed 35 percent of the adjusted gross estate.

- Liability of the stock is for payment of estate costs and taxation.

- The redemption must occur within four years of the decedent's death.

Sec. 303 generally does not recognize capital gains. This is because of the step up in value at the shareholder's death. Capital gains will only be applied on appreciation after the death of the shareholder. Sec. 303 converts what would be considered dividend income into nontaxable income.

Alternate Valuation Dates

Assets usually are valued at their fair market value on your date of death. The law provides for an alternate date to be used. If you elect this alternate date, you cannot change it; the election is irrevocable. The alternate date is six months after the decedent's date of death or the earlier date that the estate property is sold.

If your personal representative elects the alternate date, the property sold within six months of your death must be valued as of that date. If the property is not sold, it will be valued as if exchanged or distributed. This valuation will also be a fair market value as of this date.

Exercise caution in using this alternate date for valuation. Capital gains tax that would normally not apply because of the step up in basis may apply on any appreciation from the date of death to the alternate valuation date. Look at this carefully when considering the use of this alternate date.

*S*ection 303 qualifies what would ordinarily be considered dividend income and turns it into nontaxable income! ♦

SECTION 2032(a) SPECIAL USE VALUATION: FARM AND BUSINESS REAL ESTATE

Section 2032(a) is designed for the purpose of valuing *real estate* on a basis of current use rather than its highest value and best use. Certain requirements must be met to use this valuation method and it applies to *farm* and *business* real estate only. The requirements are as follows:

- The adjusted value of the farm or business property must be at least 50 percent of the adjusted value of the gross estate. The *adjusted estate* is defined as the gross estate less debts.

- The adjusted value of the real estate must be at least 25 percent of the adjusted value of the gross estate.

- The property must have been employed for farm or business purposes for at least five of the last eight years.

- The property must pass to a qualified heir. A *qualified heir* is defined as a spouse, ancestor, lineal descendants, siblings and lineal descendents of the decedent's parents.

- The decedent must have materially participated in the farm or business.

This section of the code can reduce the value of the gross estate by up to $750,000. It is designed to both reduce taxes and solve some of the liquidity problems within estates.

A detriment of this special valuation use is that if the qualified heir sells the property within ten years after the decedent's date of death, all of the estate tax savings (100 percent) will be recaptured by the IRS. The recapture provision is phased out between the 10th and 15th year following the decedent's death.

SUMMARY

Section 6166, Section 303 redemption alternate valuation dates and Section 2032(a) appear to be a relief from taxation. However, strict guidelines have to be met for each to be effective. It is because of this complexity that usage of this technique is extremely difficult to assess and is seldom used.

CHAPTER 22

Protecting Your Assets

Watching Your Backside

Over the last decade in the United States there has been an explosion in the litigation process, some of which has produced awards for damages under negligence, personal injury and malpractice suits that can only be described as absurd and exorbitant. The effects of these judgments are now being felt globally as legal precedents and award benchmarks are established and insurers withdraw from liability markets or raise premiums to unaffordable levels.

The lack of effective *tort* (wrongful act) reform and the justice system in general are now producing a substantial level of litigation against professionals, trustees, company directors and corporate executives. The recent economic recession has also heightened the awareness of the need to protect wealth with contingent creditor action.

THE U.S. LEGAL SYSTEM AND THE "DEEP POCKET" ATTITUDE

The traditional theories of legal liability and punitive damages have been expanded greatly over the years to the point that there is no serious effort at tort reform in the U.S. legal system. This expansion of legal theories has resulted in an explosion of lawsuits, especially against those who have deep pockets. The "deep pocket" attitude in today's legal society has allowed some plaintiffs and their attorneys (who otherwise would not have had a legal foundation on which to base their claims) to find incentives to sue. This devastating increase in litigation has contributed to the exorbitantly high cost of professional malpractice insurance for physicians, accountants, architects, engineers, lawyers and entrepreneurs. Often premiums are so costly that these professionals are forced to go without malpractice insurance. As a result, liability insurance is virtually nonexistent because of rampant product liability claims and the exorbitant cost of annual premiums.

The legal community has created contingency fees ranging between 33 and 40 percent of the eventual settlement. With such high fees, there is a strong economic incentive for contingency-fee law firms to file as many lawsuits as possible in the hopes that the majority will settle out of court.

The U.S. professional and businessperson has witnessed a dramatic increase in their economic loss and liability exposure due to malpractice claims and liability of third persons and ultimately judgment creditors. There has been an increase in litigation that is a direct result of the legal process and the aggressiveness of legal counsel, particularly in the United States.

There has been an increase in litigation that is a direct result of the legal process and the aggressiveness of legal counsel, particularly in the United States. ♦

Unfortunately, today professionals and companies thought to have deep pockets are frequent targets of frivolous and dubious lawsuits that are brought about with the hopes of an easy settlement. The U.S. legal system has dramatically expanded the theories of legal liability against potential defendants. This places those defendants in a very precarious legal position, often causing them large legal expenses and possible adverse judgments.

Many critics see the heart of this problem as the U.S. legal system, which has created approximately 314 attorneys per 100,000 individuals. The state of California alone has approximately 120,000 attorneys licensed to practice law. England has 112 attorneys per 100,000 people, whereas Japan has only 12 attorneys per 100,000 people. The United States by far has the largest number of attorneys, which in turn results in its being the most litigious country in the world. Furthermore, according to the American Bar Association, a lawsuit is filed in this country every 1.75 seconds.

In the January 1991 issue of *Inside* magazine, various predictions were made about the litigation explosion for the coming year. *Lawyers Alert* has the following other predictions for 1991: "Juries will hand down bigger damage awards for emotional distress and tort suits; more verdicts will come under attack because of claims of bias and jury selection; lawsuits over toxic waste cleanup will pour in from real estate agents, developers, building contractors and insurance companies trying to shift blame from themselves; and multi-million-dollar jury awards for personal injuries will become more frequent."

CAUSES FOR LITIGATION

There are many potential problems you must be aware of to avoid the litigation process. For example, here is a short list of some of the probable causes for litigation:

- Problems relating to your home or commercial property, including loose gravel, wet sidewalks, clean glass windows, uneven pavement, doors that people walk through, swimming pools and open gates

- Accidents caused by your children

- Accidents or incidents caused by someone in your employ or by a subcontractor, including auto accidents while on company business or potential harassment

- Auto accidents

- Equipment malfunctions

- Recreational outing accidents

- Professional malpractice

- Slips and falls on commercial property

- Exposure as a director or officer of a corporation

ASSET PROTECTION PLANNING

The following are just a few examples that illustrate why *asset protection planning* has become a crucial part of estate planning.

Example

A woman who was a customer of a Florida furniture company was awarded $2.5 million, which the furniture company had to pay after its deliveryman stabbed her. The court ruled that the company had failed to do elaborate screening when they hired the deliveryman and held that the company was liable for negligence.

Example

Consider the case of a family in Escondido, California, who owned an auto repair business. Ten years before the state of California imposed a $7.9 million order upon the family, they had a disposal company remove hazardous materials from the property owned by the family. The state of California declared the yard site unsafe, and the removal company subsequently filed bankruptcy. As a result, California imposed a fine of $7.9 million on the family and their legal next of kin. Even though the family had made strenuous efforts to work within the state's environmental guidelines, California still imposed this large penalty.

Example

The case of Mrs. W. illustrates that litigation fever can affect anyone. Mrs. W. loaned her 18-year-old grand-nephew $18,000 to buy a used 1981 Chrysler. After a long party that, according to court records, included smoking marijuana and drinking, the grandnephew and his friends started driving the car, subsequently lost control of it and drove off a railroad bridge. As a result, one of the passengers lost his leg in the accident and was paralyzed from the chest down. The paralyzed passenger subsequently sued Mrs. W., and a jury found the 91-year-old woman liable to the paralyzed patient. The court ordered her to pay the paralyzed passenger $950,000!

PREVENTING LITIGATION WITH ASSET PROTECTION PLANNING

The businessperson and the professional in the United States has for years utilized two concepts to maintain and create wealth: (1) financial planning and (2) estate planning. These two types of planning are primarily concerned with building and maintaining one's estate. The third type of planning has been developed to minimize the risk of economic loss exposure due to the litigious nature of our society. This type of planning, called *asset protection planning,* utilizes various techniques in protecting assets from potential creditors. The key to asset protection planning is the preventive planning that occurs *before* creditors file claims.

The people who are more prone to potential litigation are physicians, surgeons, dentists, financial planners, investment advisers, attorneys, accountants, natural resource developers, manufacturers, developers, architects, contractors, insurance agents, board directors, entrepreneurs and real estate owners.

These individuals can minimize the risk of exposure through various techniques to protect their assets from potential creditors. The key to such planning is *preventive* asset protection planning, rather than trying to protect assets when a creditor already has a judgment or lawsuit against the individual or business.

The concept behind litigation in today's society is based on economic factors and not necessarily on the pursuit of justice. Before a plaintiff's attorney institutes a major lawsuit against a defendant, there is an investigation into the defendant's ability to pay the claim; if there are no funds to sue for, no legal action will be taken by the plaintiff. If you become an unattractive target of a lawsuit, then you and your assets will more than likely not be subject to litigation in the future. The primary goal of asset protection is to render unattractive the assets that were once attractive to the potential plaintiff through the use of various asset protection techniques.

Asset protection is a process where a person divests himself or herself of legal ownership of particular assets that are vulnerable to judgment creditors while at the same time maintaining or regaining control of those assets for his or her use and enjoyment. The process of asset protection planning and the establishment of the various asset protection planning techniques and strategies must be made in advance of any claims by creditors. Asset protection planning cannot be done at the 11th hour or after a creditor has obtained a judgment or filed a claim against an individual.

Before an asset protection plan can be recommended and begun, it is necessary to evaluate the entire estate. Asset planning strategies typically are structured around particular assets, whether they be cash, bonds, stocks, business interests, insurance proceeds, jewelry, art, antiques, real property, etc. Those particular assets that are considered nonexempt by state and federal law are the most vulnerable assets in a lawsuit and in the minds of judgment creditors. Therefore, the concept behind asset protection planning is to protect particular assets within an individual's estate from claims by creditors and judgment creditors rather than protecting the individual from lawsuits.

The first caveat of asset protection planning is that there is *no absolute technique or techniques* to fully protect your assets from potential creditors. In light of this, the objective of asset protection is to create a legal fortress around an individual's assets such that it is impractical for creditors to penetrate.

*T*he first caveat of asset protection planning is that there is *no absolute technique or techniques* to fully protect your assets from potential creditors. ♦

OTHER BENEFITS OF ASSET PROTECTION PLANS

As a result of creating this financial fortress, other benefits arise. There are many practical applications of asset protection.

- Replacement or supplement to liability insurance
- Means to provide backup coverage
- Protection from activities outside the main area of work
- Reduction of financial profile so as to discourage suits
- Segregation of wealth so not all assets are in one investment/instrument
- Protection of retirement benefits
- Establishment of a dispositive estate plan
- An increase in strategic position with respect to negotiations with present creditors
- Discouragement of potential creditors from filing lawsuits
- Privacy of financial affairs
- More cost-efficient than litigation

REQUIREMENTS FOR CREATING AN ASSET PROTECTION PLAN

It is very important that you meet the following requirements in order to establish an asset protection plan:

- You must be solvent at the date assets are transferred to the trust.
- Your motivation and intent cannot be to avoid creditors.
- There may be no intent to make a fraudulent transfer.
- You must make a full disclosure to the IRS.

The legal system has recently witnessed the erosion of traditional legal techniques to limited and individual liability. Within certain states the rights of creditors against these techniques have been expanded to the extent that the legal practitioner has searched out new and more effective ways to protect assets from creditors and judgment creditors. We will focus on two techniques (the family limited partnership and foreign trust planning) that can be utilized and that we have found to be extremely effective, not only for asset protection but for estate planning purposes.

THE FAMILY LIMITED PARTNERSHIP

A family limited partnership is a better domestic technique for protection against potential creditors than any other domestic instrument used for asset protection, such as a domestic corporation. ♦

The **family limited partnership** is a unique entity that provides ultimate control and management of partnership assets while at the same time providing asset protection benefits. In a family limited partnership, there are one or more general partners who are vested with the management control of partnership affairs and assets. Limited partners, of which there can be one or more, do not have any control or management in partnership affairs or the management of assets. The limited partner's role is passive and therefore has limited liability for the obligations of the partnership.

A family limited partnership is a better domestic technique for protection against potential creditors than any other domestic instrument used for asset protection, such as a domestic corporation. Once a creditor obtains a judgment against you as a general partner, he or she must obtain a *charging order* against your partnership interest, giving them an interest only in the income of the partnership rather than the principal. This is very limited since the judgment creditor now must pay income taxes on the undistributed profits and income of the partnership in proportion to his or her interest as determined by the charging order, even if no income is distributed by the partnership.

Thus, the judgment creditor becomes an assignee and is liable for taxation on income that he or she does not receive. The partnership agreement is drafted in such a way as to give the general partner the discretion to distribute income to the limited partners. This then becomes a definite barrier to a plaintiff's attorney when determining to file suit against you.

Supervision is written into the family limited partnership in that the general partner or partners have the power to make or not make partnership distributions. Thus, in the event that there is a charging order against the partner's share in the partnership, the general partner can effectively turn off the income stream to that partner and allow the income to accumulate and be reinvested within the partnership. Thus, if the debtor partner does not actually receive income, the judgment creditor with the charging order will not receive income as well. What is typically done in this case is the general partner distributes to the debtor partner the exact amount of tax to be paid for the partner's distributions so the debtor partner may pay the tax without having to come up with the funds out of his or her own pocket. Therefore, if the debtor partner must pay tax on partnership income, whether he or she receives it or not, the law states that a judgment creditor with a charging order must pay tax on the partnership distribution whether the judgment creditor receives it or not.

If a family limited partnership itself becomes subject to a lawsuit, all the assets within that partnership will become subject to the claims with the creditor. Negative circumstances can potentially occur if an asset within the partnership can cause liability. For example, a tort claim will most likely happen due to a faulty apartment complex that has not been maintained for years. Under this circumstance, it is best to segregate out from the estate any particular asset or assets that may cause liability in and of themselves and place the asset or assets in separate family limited partnerships. This technique is often used if you own separate commercial buildings or apartment buildings. Each apartment building would be transferred to a separate family limited partnership. If there is a slip-and-fall case on one of the apartment building premises, the separate family limited partnership that holds the particular apartment building would be subject to the plaintiff's claims, and the other apartment buildings within the estate would be free from liability.

PARTICULAR STRUCTURES UTILIZING THE FAMILY LIMITED PARTNERSHIP

Figures 22.1 through 22.6 illustrate examples of particular asset protection structures that utilize the family limited partnership.

Structure 1: Husband and Wife as Limited Partners

In Figure 22.1, husband and wife form a family partnership in which the husband holds a 1 percent interest as general partner and the wife holds a 1 percent interest as general partner. As limited partners, the husband owns 49 percent and the wife owns 49 percent.

This particular structure is useful for assets that do not generate a large amount of income. This is because if a creditor were to sue the vulnerable spouse (e.g., the husband who is a doctor), he or she would be able to seize through a charging order any distributions to the husband but not the wife.

FIGURE 22.1 Family Limited Partnership Structure 1: Husband and Wife as Limited Partners

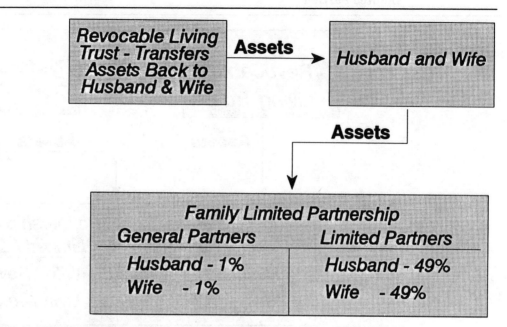

Structure 2: Less Vulnerable Spouse as Limited Partner

If the husband and wife held income-producing assets that generated income used to support necessary expenses, the structure in Figure 22.2 would be useful. In this structure the husband and wife form a limited partnership in which each has a 1 percent interest as general partners. The other 98 percent is held by the wife—i.e., the less vulnerable spouse—as a limited partner. No gift tax implications apply from this particular transaction since the gift of the husband's interest in the asset is considered an interspousal transfer and thus free from gift tax taxation.

If a creditor pursued the vulnerable spouse—i.e., the husband/doctor—the creditor would only have the right to the 1 percent interest through a charging order. The other 99 percent distributed to the wife would not be attachable by the creditor and could be used to pay expenses.

Structure 3: Children as Limited Partners

If both spouses have a child or children who are adults and both spouses are vulnerable to lawsuits, they may want to form a family limited partnership in which each spouse holds a 1 percent interest as general partners and the remaining 98

FIGURE 22.2   Family Limited Partnership Structure 2: Less Vulnerable Spouse as Limited Partner

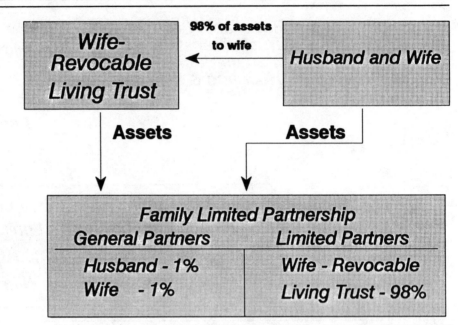

percent of the partnership is held among their children or a child in the proportion that they desire. If, for example, the spouses have two children, they can donate their $1 million in commercial property to their children in the form of limited partnership units—i.e., 49 units or 49 percent to each child. (See Figure 22.3.) This particular structure may trigger a gift tax liability but could be offset with the spouses' combined $1.2 million exemption, depending upon how much credit has been previously used.

The children now own the commercial property, the assets to be protected, as limited partners in a family limited partnership that is managed and controlled by the parents.

Structure 4: Irrevocable Trust as Limited Partner

Suppose both spouses are vulnerable to lawsuits. In this instance the husband and wife could form a family limited partnership in which each owns a 1 percent interest as general partners, thus maintaining management control of the underlying assets (see Figure 22.4).

The husband and wife would then settle (create) an irrevocable trust, naming themselves as trustees and their children as beneficiaries. The husband and wife would then transfer the income-producing assets into the trust for the benefit of their children. The trustee of the irrevocable trust—i.e., the husband

FIGURE 22.3   Family Limited Partnership Structure 3: Children as Limited Partners

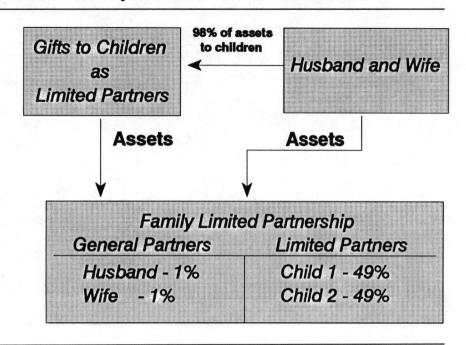

and wife—would then become a 98 percent limited partner in the family limited partnership.

If husband and wife, who are both vulnerable to lawsuits, were sued and a judgment was rendered against both of them, the judgment creditor could obtain only a charging order against the 1 percent interest they hold as general partners and not against the 98 percent held by the trustee of the irrevocable trust. Therefore, the judgment creditor would not be entitled to any partnership income distributed by the general partners to the trustee (the husband and wife) of the irrevocable trust.

Structure 5: Foreign Trust as Limited Partner

One particular structure that has proven useful is the foreign asset protection trust and family limited partnership (see Figure 22.5). If you are reluctant to transfer assets offshore to a foreign jurisdiction that is held by a foreign trustee, you can establish a family limited partnership in which you are a 1 percent general partner with complete management control over the assets. The 99 percent limited partnership is then transferred to a foreign trust. Under partnership law, a limited partner does not have any right to management control over partnership assets. Therefore, the foreign trustee is a substi-

FIGURE 22.4 Family Limited Partnership Structure 4: Irrevocable Trust as Limited Partner

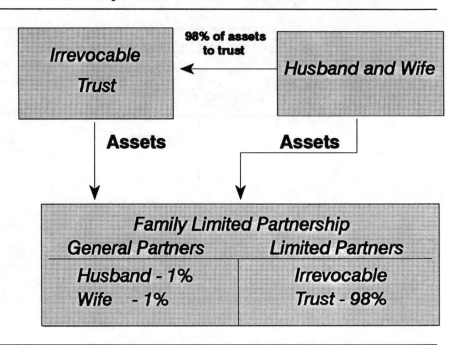

tute limited partner and is free from any management control over the underlying asset.

This particular structure is excellent for real estate, which, of course, is a nonmovable asset, even though liquid assets such as cash and securities can be utilized in this structure. In fact, what you have created is a structure in which you control and manage the assets to be protected whereby title is held by a foreign trustee in a foreign jurisdiction and the assets remain in the United States. This provides ultimate control for a client; assets are legally held by the partnership and not the foreign trustee. All that the foreign trustee owns is a limited partnership interest in the family limited partnership.

This particular structure is an excellent technique to avoid possible claims by judgment creditors to foreclose upon the debtor partner's interest in the partnership.

Structure 6: The Foreign Asset Protection Trust (FAPT)

The utilization of the *foreign asset protection trust (FAPT)* can provide unparalleled protection of assets over and above the use of the family limited partnership.

The FAPT is simply a revocable living trust established under the laws of a foreign country that has favorable asset protection legislation, such as the Cook Islands in the South Pacific, the island of Madeira or the Republic of Mauritius in

FIGURE 22.5   Family Limited Partnership Structure 5: Foreign Asset Protection Trust

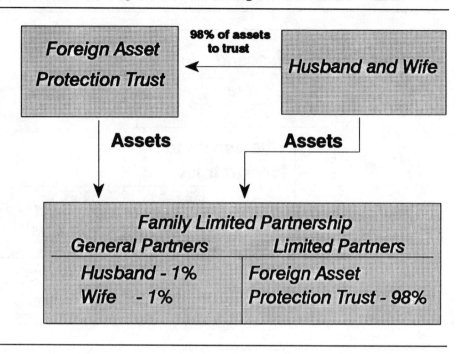

the Indian Ocean. Incorporated into the FAPT are various provisions that take advantage of asset protection legislation. The FAPT also can be used in conjunction with other estate planning techniques and in estate tax planning.

FAPTs are tax neutral and should not be used to evade U.S. taxes. The specific structure of a properly drafted FAPT should provide no tax benefits or liabilities. The trust should be exempt from the Internal Revenue Code 1491 excise tax of 35 percent on real estate and the underlying corporation is domestic rather than offshore.

The foreign trustee, as the 100 percent shareholder of the underlying corporation, holds a shareholder's meeting in which it appoints the board of directors or director. The trustee as shareholder appoints you as the sole director responsible for operating the corporation on a day-to-day basis. Another option is for you to enter into a consulting agreement with the underlying corporation instead of becoming a director. Still another option is for you to have power of attorney over the underlying corporation. Directors' fees, management fees or consultation fees can be arranged between you and the underlying corporation. This structure results in you regaining and maintaining control of the assets being protected. (See Figure 22.6.)

You may wish to utilize an FAPT alone. You create the FAPT in a jurisdiction that has favorable asset protection legislation (e.g., the Republic of Mauritius). You then appoint a foreign

FIGURE 22.6 Family Limited Partnership Structure 6: Foreign Asset Protection Trust

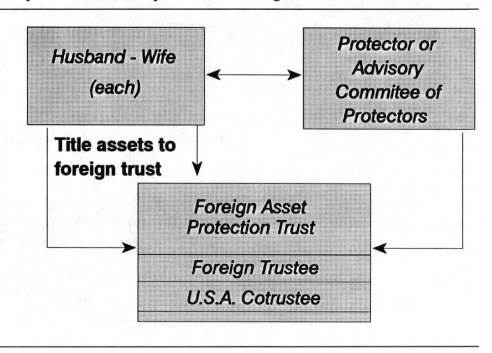

independent trustee to hold and manage the underlying assets of the trust.

Since the FAPT is irrevocable and the settlor cannot exercise control of the underlying assets, he or she may wish to appoint either a U.S. cotrustee, protector or advisory committee of protectors.

Asset protection planning is a highly specialized area of law. We have found few law firms in the United States that deal with these issues. If you are considering this type of planning, we recommend that you find a firm that specializes in this area even if this means traveling out of state. We welcome you to call our 800 numbers (see the information at the end of this book) to receive further information on firms that are in your area or that specialize in this area of law. In addition, please call and request our special report entitled "Asset Protection Strategies for the '90s."

CHAPTER 23

Getting Started: Taking the Next Step

Our Invitation to You

Take this simple test. For a few moments close your eyes and think about the potential problems that would arise if you died today. Try to answer some of the following questions:

- How will my estate pass to my family or heirs?

- Will family members have enough income to continue with their accustomed lifestyles?

- Can the business continue without me?

- Will those to whom I want to leave my estate actually receive it?

- Who will gain guardianship of my (minor) children?

- Will my estate be subject to probate?

- How much will my estate have to pay in federal estate taxation and other costs?

- What transformations will my estate have to go through to pay the tax bill?

These are just a few of the common questions that death creates; the list goes on and on.

WHERE DO YOU START?

To come up with an estate plan, where do you start? Having facilitated hundreds of estate plans, we recommend that you find an estate planning quarterback—a person who can summarize your current estate planning (if any is in place); identify problems; and help you set objectives, format and execute a plan.

To begin the process, you must first make a choice. Who would you like to inherit your estate? Your children and other heirs or the federal government, the state government and the legal system? If you are like most people, the answer is simple. However, ensuring that your choice becomes a reality is not so easy.

Unfortunately, the harsh reality is that government and the legal system are set up to get your money and make it their money.

Somehow, much of what the United States stands for has been twisted like a pretzel. We have lost sight of the premise that we are a free society that allows and encourages its citizens to become successful. Why does it now follow that having a high income and net worth makes you a bad person, one who is considered greedy and money hungry?

In our estimation there has been a reversal in the psychology of the public because of the hard times we've been through in the past few years. The recession of the early 1990s fostered a sense of jealousy and created, as Dr. Gary North coined it, "an age of envy." Although it is called a recession, we think it's much more of a deep, fundamental change in the structure of our economy. It is now politically correct to say that anyone who has the audacity to make a lot of money should pay for their "crimes." And the government will do this by "taxing the heck out of you."

Sadly, the federal system is not alone in the effort to reduce your net worth. Much of the legal system stands to gain from your wealth as well.

Therefore, you need to organize your financial affairs so that you pay the least amount of legal fees, along with the lowest taxes possible. The government and legal system do not profit unless your affairs are disorganized and vulnerable to an exorbitant tax bill. The legal system is designed so that an attorney's motivation is often different from your own.

Between the reality of the current political climate, the likelihood of increases in federal estate taxation and the lack of incentive for the legal system to organize your affairs accurately, holding onto your assets is more difficult than ever. What does this mean to you? It means that you need to plan now for the future.

*U*nfortunately, the harsh reality is that government and the legal system are set up to get your money and make it their money. ♦

*T*he government and legal system do not profit unless your affairs are disorganized and vulnerable to an exorbitant tax bill. ♦

♦ **WARNING**　　Estate planning is no longer an option; it is a necessity.

The following situations are standard occurrences in our society:

Example

Sam is a 64-year-old corporate executive. His wife Janet is also 64 and not employed, having been active in charitable organizations most of her adult life. Sam plans on retiring at 65. He has been with the same large corporation for the last 24 years. Over the course of his career, Sam has paid as much as 60 percent of his annual earnings in federal and state income taxation. Sam and Janet are currently in a 43 percent tax bracket. For each dollar Sam makes, they are able to keep only 57 cents.

Sam and Janet have accumulated assets valued at $3.5 million. These assets include the value of Sam's qualified retirement program (approximately $1.5 million). Under current law, if both Sam and Janet die today, their federal estate tax will be $1,535,000 before any other person or heir receives a penny. The IRS will require the estate to pay this tax, in cash, within nine months after their deaths.

Their tax loss can be measured, and with proper planning they can avoid the ravages inflicted upon a poorly planned estate. *Estate taxes and huge legal bills are not necessary.* With proper planning, the estate taxes and legal fees for Sam and Janet can be minimal!

Example

Tom and Frances started their manufacturing company in Seattle almost 20 years ago. The gross annual sales of the company are approximately $2.5 million. Tom's son Greg has been involved in the business for about 15 years. Two other children are not involved in the business and live out of state.

Today Tom is 67 years old and wants to retire. He has thought about selling the company in order to retire but hasn't for two important reasons. First, Greg's hard work and determination have helped build the Tom James Company to its current level of success. Greg shares his father's desire to keep the business in the family and to one day pass it on to his own children. Second, if Tom sells the business, he will face a capital gains tax on the sale of approximately $1.3 million.

Tom's net interest in the company is valued at about $3.5 million. If Tom dies today, the federal estate tax on the value of his estate (including his business interest) will be about $2.5 million. Tom's estate has very few liquid assets to pay this liability. It is also true that the company has very little cash to redeem Tom's stock.

Tom is concerned that the tax liability could severely impact the future operations of the business, not to mention the income outlook for Frances, if she survives him. He would like to leave the business intact for Greg and Greg's family and wants to leave his other children and grandchildren an equivalent amount of inheritance.

Tom and Frances recognize the potential problems with the company and their estate but don't know where to start to solve them.

We have covered many techniques that a family can utilize to reduce or even eliminate estate taxes and legal costs.

- You can remove hundreds of thousands of dollars from your taxable estate, while retaining the ability to receive income from the assets.

- You can work with your family to reduce your taxable estate without losing control of it.

- You can discount the value of your stock in your company, using methods most planners are unaware of.

- You can leave millions of dollars to your grandchildren, saving hundreds of thousands of dollars in estate taxes in the process.

These options allow you to save hundreds of thousands, even millions, of dollars in estate taxes and legal fees.

You may wonder why your CPA and attorney haven't discussed these opportunities with you. We have found that if professional advisers do not specialize in the practice of estate planning, they will be vague on the techniques that we have outlined. In addition, a good portion of these professionals spend their time correcting the past, not planning for the future. When was the last time your accountant showed how you could save in future income tax? Generally they tell you only what is due and make certain that it is paid before they sign the return.

This area of tax planning is very complex, and many professionals who do not specialize in estate planning don't have the time and the expertise to facilitate your estate plan correctly.

If you don't effectively plan your estate, any one of the following can happen:

- Your family can lose thousands of dollars to estate taxes and spend tens of thousands of dollars on unnecessary legal fees.

- In the event of your death or disability, your family may be left without any direction from you on how to proceed.

- Your heirs may be forced to sell assets to create liquidity for estate taxes.

- The transfer of your estate can be a financial and emotional nightmare.

A well-planned estate will pass to your heirs in its entirety, in the manner you design. Therefore, you should seek assistance from a professional planner who can help you through the maze of estate planning options.

Figure 23.1 contains a very simple personal estate planning profile. This profile (or an equivalent profile) is the basis for starting your estate planning. It will allow an estate planner to determine fundamental problems where there is no existing estate plan, amend problems with current plans that have been recently executed or update plans that have been in place for many years.

THE NEXT STEP: CREATING YOUR OWN ESTATE PLAN

Completing your personal estate planning profile is an important first step. Our offer to you is to help you create an effective estate plan that will allow you to achieve your goals. If you do not have an estate planner and are just beginning the process of planning, we offer you an estate planning summary of your current estate at the end of this book.

This detailed summary serves several purposes. It will

- identify probate assets and multiple probate assets;

- assess probate costs;

- calculate federal estate tax liability at your death and then at the death of a surviving spouse;

- identify how assets are owned and give comparisons of alternative ownership;

- identify specific problems, such as a lack of liquidity for federal estate tax liability, and outline ways to correct these problems;

- assess current gifting strategies and suggest ways to improve these strategies; and

- identify specific problems as outlined in the text of this book and format strategies to solve these problems in a clear, concise and detailed report.

*T*he best time to have planned your estate was yesterday; but if you failed to complete your planning yesterday, then *today* is the second-best time to start. ♦

If you already have an estate plan in place but have not implemented the strategies described in this book (e.g., the 1 percent solution) and you would like actual numbers or illustrations on any of the outlined strategies in Part II, you may call our toll-free numbers (800-598-9406 or 800-223-9610) and request the information by phone or fill out the survey form at the back of the book.

The problems that are created at death are devastating. The best time to have planned your estate was yesterday; but if you failed to complete your planning yesterday, then *today* is the second-best time to start.

Figure 23.2 illustrates why procrastination can become a problem. It doesn't have to happen to you!

FIGURE 23.1 Personal Estate Planning Profile Fact Sheet

PERSONAL ESTATE PLANNING PROFILE
CONFIDENTIAL

IF YOU ARE SINGLE, WIDOWED OR DIVORCED, SIMPLY PROVIDE YOUR PERSONAL INFORMATION
AND DISREGARD ALL REFERENCES TO A SPOUSE.

CLIENT'S FULL NAME			CLIENT'S FULL NAME (Spouse)		
DATE OF BIRTH	CITIZENSHIP	OCCUPATION	DATE OF BIRTH	CITIZENSHIP	OCCUPATION

HOME ADDRESS	CITY, STATE, ZIP	HOME PHONE ( )
MAILING ADDRESS	CITY, STATE, ZIP	WORK PHONE ( )

ASSETS AND LIABILITIES

HOW IS TITLE HELD? **KEY :** H=Husband's separate W=Wife's separate

CP=Community property RLT= Revocable Living Trust
JT=Joint tenancy TC= Tenancy in common
TE=Tenancy by entirety

DESCRIPTION OF ASSETS	FAIR MARKET VALUE	LIABILITY	NET VALUE	HOW IS TITLE HELD?
RESIDENCE				
OTHER REAL ESTATE				
STOCKS AND BONDS				
BUSINESS INTERESTS				
CASH IN BANKS (CD(s), MONEY MARKETS)				
NOTES RECEIVABLE				
PERSONAL EFFECTS (AUTOS, BOATS, ETC.)				
RETIREMENT PLAN (NOT IN SETTLEMENT)				
OTHER ASSETS				
OTHER DEBTS				
TOTALS:				

LIFE INSURANCE & ANNUITIES (Please list additional policies on separate paper.)

COMPANY	INSURED	OWNER	BENEFICIARY	FACE AMOUNT	CASH VALUE

INCOME
JOINT ANNUAL GROSS EARNED INCOME $ _____   JOINT ANNUAL GROSS INCOME FROM INVESTMENTS $ _____

CHILDREN (LIST ALL LIVING CHILDREN: C=CLIENT S=SPOUSE J=JOINT)

NAME	AGE	SEX M F	PARENT C S J	NAME	AGE	SEX M F	PARENT C S J
NAME	AGE	SEX M F	PARENT C S J	NAME	AGE	SEX M F	PARENT C S J

GRANDCHILDREN (INDICATE SAME AS FOR CHILDREN)

NAME	AGE	SEX M F	GRANDPARENT C S J	NOTES:
NAME	AGE	SEX M F	GRANDPARENT C S J	

FIGURE 23.2 Procrastination Will Be Dangerous to Your Wealth

Don't Let This Happen to You

Glossary

adjusted gross estate The gross estate less debts, administration expenses and losses during administration.

adjusted taxable estate The adjusted gross estate less any marital and/or charitable deduction.

adjusted taxable gifts Gifts that exceed the unified credit or $600,000 exemption and the annual gift tax exclusion. Gifted amounts over and above the exemption and annual exclusion at death are added back to the taxable estate and are subject to estate tax.

administration The formal process of settling an estate. Various duties include valuing the estate, filing tax returns, paying taxes and distributing assets to heirs.

administration expenses Expenses incurred while administering an estate. These include legal fees, appraisal fees, distribution and disposition costs.

after-born child A child born after the death of a parent.

alternate valuation date A date used by the personal representative to value a decedent's estate. This date is not to exceed six months after date of death. The value of the assets must be lower and result in a reduction of the gross estate and a reduction in the estate tax liability to qualify for its use.

annual gift tax exclusion The right of each individual to make small annual gifts to other individuals each year to the extent of $10,000 (under current law). The number of these gifts is unlimited. These small annual gifts are in addition to the unified credit or $600,000 exemption equivalent amount. They do not reduce the unified credit or exemption equivalent.

ascertainable standards   Involves the right of a surviving spouse to invade the family trust or B trust without causing the property to be included in his or her estate. The power is limited to standards such as needs for health, education, maintenance and support.

basis   The original amount paid to acquire an asset or the fair market value of an asset on the date it was acquired.

beneficiary   The persons and/or organizations who receive the trust property after the death of the trust grantor. Also refers to those who receive property under a contract (such as an annuity or life insurance policy) through a beneficiary designation.

bequest   A *specific* bequest is a gift by will of a designated class or kind of property (e.g., a gift of the descendent's residence to a named individual). A *general* bequest is one that is accomplished from the general assets of an estate (e.g., a bequest of a sum of money without reference to any particular account or investment from which it is to be distributed).

book value   In valuing businesses, book value equals assets less liabilities. It is the net worth of the business.

B trust   A trust created at death under a provision in the will (testamentary) or by provision in a trust. This trust is often referred to as the *family trust* and usually holds the unified credit or exemption equivalent amount (in spousal estates) of the first spouse to die. It also qualifies assets placed into the trust for the use of the unified credit.

bypass trust   A trust designed not to qualify for the unlimited estate tax marital deduction. This trust, commonly referred to as the *family trust* or *B trust,* is designed to make use of the lifetime $600,000 exclusion (unified credit).

capitalization of earnings   When valuing a business, this is the measure of earning capacity.

charitable deduction   A deduction allowed for a gift to a qualified charitable organization.

charitable gifting Gifts of cash or other assets made to (under the IRS definition) qualified charities for which the donor receives various tax deductions.

charitable remainder trust (CRT) The donation of property or money to a charity, where the donor reserves the right to use the property or to receive income from it for a specified time. When the agreed-upon period is over, the property belongs to the charitable organization. The donor in turn receives various tax deductions and tax advantages. The most common CRTs are the charitable remainder annuity trust (CRAT) and the charitable remainder unit trust (CRUT).

codicil A revision, change or modification to an existing will.

community owned property Property acquired during marriage in which both husband and wife have an undivided one-half interest. Not more than one-half of community property can be disposed of by the will. There are currently nine community property states: Arizona, California, Idaho, Louisiana, New Mexico, Nevada, Texas, Washington and Wisconsin.

corpus The principal property of a trust. Separate from trust income, it is property transferred to the trust. (Also referred to as *principal*.)

credit estate tax A state death tax imposed to take full advantage of the amount allowed as a credit against the federal estate tax.

crummy power The power held by the beneficiary of a trust to withdraw a certain amount annually from the trust. This amount is limited to $5,000 or 5 percent of the trust corpus each year.

curtesy A life estate to which a man is entitled to all property held or owned by his wife through common law. (See also **dower.**)

death tax Tax imposed by the federal government that can be in excess of 55 percent and tax that is imposed by some state governments.

deemed transferor The parent of the transferee most closely related to the grantor. A parent related to the grantor by blood or adoption is deemed closer than one related by marriage. This relationship is important in understanding the taxation of generation-skipping transfers.

devise Legally, a gift of real estate under a will, as distinguished from a gift of personal property.

direct skip The transfer of assets or gifts made directly to second-generation beneficiaries, skipping the middle generation. For example, gifts made by a grandfather to a grandchild while skipping the grandfather's children.

domicile State and place of official residence.

donee The recipient of a gift. This may also refer to the recipient of a power of appointment. Refers to an individual or entity capable of owning property.

donor A person who makes a gift or grants a power of appointment. Limited to individuals only.

dower A woman's entitlement to an interest in all the property of her husband that was owned during their marriage.

dynasty trust An irrevocable life insurance trust (ILIT) used by wealthy people to create nontaxable generation-skipping transfers to several generations.

Economic Recovery Tax Act of 1981 (ERTA) A broad-based tax reform legislation signed into law under the Reagan administration. This legislation, as it pertains to estate planning, created the unlimited marital deduction, increased the estate and gift tax exemption and restructured the estate and gift tax rates.

estate analysis A formal written estate plan that analyzes estate taxation, property ownership, probate costs, current planning, etc. and formulates a plan to achieve various objectives. It is a road map for achieving the objectives, format and execution of an effective estate plan.

estate freeze Methods whereby highly appreciating assets are shifted out of an estate so that future appreciation will not be included in the gross estate. These include business as well as personal assets.

estate planners Individuals who specialize and devote 100 percent of their time to the issues and practice of planning estates. Backgrounds can vary from attorneys to financial service professionals.

estate tax A tax imposed upon the right of a person to transfer property at death. This tax may be imposed not only by the federal government but also by state governments. The transfer tax is generally applicable to estates valued over and above the $600,000 exemption amount.

estate tax base An amount determined by subtracting the allowable expenses, deductions and exclusions from the gross estate and adding back in any adjusted taxable gifts. This is the amount on which the federal estate tax is levied.

estate-tax states Those states that impose a death tax direct to the estate and do not share in revenues collected by the federal government.

excess accumulations estate tax A 15 percent additional estate tax imposed on qualified retirement plans as a penalty for overfunding these plans and not taking IRS guideline distributions.

excess distribution tax A 15 percent penalty tax on excessive distributions from a qualified retirement plan.

exemption equivalent The unified credit amount (currently $600,000) that is exempt from estate and gift taxes. Each individual is allowed this exemption.

fair market value The value at which estate property is included in the gross estate for federal estate tax purposes. The price at which property would change hands between a willing buyer and a willing seller under any compulsion to buy or sell and both having knowledge of all the relevant facts.

family allowance Money available from an estate for the testator's spouse and children while the estate is being settled.

family limited partnership A legal entity that provides ultimate control and management of assets, while at the same time providing asset protection.

family trust (See **B trust**.)

federal estate tax An excise tax levied by the federal government on the right to transfer property at death. This tax is imposed upon and measured by the value of the estate left behind by the deceased.

fee simple Outright ownership of property with absolute rights to dispose of or gift it to anyone at death.

fiduciary A person in the position of great trust and responsibility, such as the executor of a will or the trustee of a trust.

five and five power A provision that allows a trust beneficiary to withdraw the greater of $5,000 or 5 percent of the principal from a trust without causing the entire trust property to be included in his or her estate for federal estate taxation.

foreign asset protection trust A revocable living trust established under the laws of a foreign country.

foreign death tax credit A credit against estate and gift taxes on an amount that is paid to foreign governments as a death tax.

formal written estate plan summary (See **estate analysis**.)

format The planning tools used in the process of estate planning. Trusts, wills, CRTs, etc. are all estate-planning formats.

funded insurance trust An insurance trust provided with income-producing property, the income from which is used to pay the premiums on the policies held in the trust.

future interest The postponed right of use or enjoyment of property.

gap-tax state Another name for states that are death tax credit states and how they determine and collect death taxes.

generation-skipping transfer (GST) A transfer of property, usually in trust, that is designed to provide benefits for two or more generations of beneficiaries who are younger than the generation of the grantor.

generation-skipping transfer tax (GSTT) A transfer tax generally assessed on gifts in excess of $1 million to grandchildren, great-grandchildren or others at least two generations below the donor.

gift splitting A provision allowing a married couple to treat a gift made by one of them to a third party as having been made as one-half by each, provided it is consented to by the other on a gift tax return.

gift tax marital deduction A deduction allowed for a gift made by one spouse to another. Outright gifts and life estates qualify for the deduction if the donee has the right to the income from the property for life and a general power of appointment over the principal. Certain qualified terminable interest gifts also qualify. The amount of the deduction is unlimited.

grantor The person who establishes the trust. Also called the *creator, settlor, donor* or *trustor.*

gross estate The total value of all property in which a deceased had an interest. This must be included in his or her estate for federal tax purposes.

guardian A person appointed to have custody over the person or the property or both of a minor or incapacitated person.

health, education, maintenance and support (HEMS) (See **ascertainable standards.**)

heir A person who is entitled to inherit assets of the decedent when the decedent left no will. Also specified as *next of kin*.

holographic will A will written entirely in the testator's own handwriting.

inheritance tax A tax imposed by a number of states based on the value of the property that taxpayers inherit. It is levied on the right to receive property, not on the right to transfer property.

insurance trust A trust established to own insurance policies in order to prevent them from being included in an estate.

intangible property Property that does not have physical value, such as a stock certificate or savings bond.

inter vivos trust A trust created during a person's lifetime. It operates during that person's lifetime as opposed to a testamentary trust, which does not operate until the grantor dies. Also called a *living trust*.

intestacy laws Individual state laws regarding the distribution of the property of a person who dies without leaving a valid will.

intestate A person who dies without having a valid will. That person dies *intestate*.

irrevocable life insurance trust (ILIT) A trust that cannot be changed or cancelled once it is created.

irrevocable trusts A trust created for the permanent transfer of property.

joint-and-last-survivor life insurance A relatively new type of life insurance that provides an insurance benefit at the death of the surviving spouse or partner. Generally, this method of providing estate liquidity for married couples is the most cost-effective strategy. Also known as survivorship insurance, second-to-die insurance.

joint ownership Occurs when two or more people own the same property. The death of a joint owner immediately transfers ownership to the surviving joint owner(s).

joint tenancy Ownership shared with an unlimited number of individuals. Each tenant owns an equal undivided share of the property.

joint tenancy with rights of survivorship (JTWRS) The holding of property by two or more individuals in a manner that upon the death of one tenant, the survivor(s) succeed to full ownership by operation of law.

lapse The failure of a bequest in a will because the intended recipient died before the testator.

last will and testament The usual formal term referring to a will.

legacy A gift of personal property by will. Usually referred to as a *bequest* in today's usage. The recipient is called the *legatee.*

leverage A true cost discount in which you can pay a few dollars now to create a significantly larger sum later.

leveraged dollars The present use of a sum of money to create a true discount in the future. Using current premium dollars now to create a large amount of dollars in the future in life insurance contracts.

life estate The title to the income interest vested in a life tenant.

life insurance Is customarily used to discount actual tax liability. For estate liquidity purposes one should acquire permanent protection.

life interest or life estate An interest that a person has in property enjoyed only during life.

life tenant The person who receives the income from a legal life estate or from a trust fund during his own life or that of another person. Often referred to as the *income beneficiary.*

limited power of appointment A special power granted to a donee that is limited in scope as opposed to being general.

liquid assets Cash or assets that can be easily converted into cash without any serious loss, such as bonds, life insurance proceeds paid in a lump sum, bank accounts and CDs.

liquidity The measure of liquid assets. In estate planning it is detrimental to measure the amount of liquid assets for the use of paying death taxes and expenses.

living trust (See **revocable living trust.**)

marital deduction The portion of a deceased spouse's estate that may be passed to the surviving spouse without becoming subject to the federal estate tax.

marital trust A trust consisting of the property that qualifies for the marital deduction.

multiple probate Property owned by a decedent in states other than the state of domicile that will be subject to probate. Usually refers to real estate owned in several states that becomes subject to each individual state's probate system at time of death.

net taxable estate The total value of an estate after all deductions have been subtracted.

nonliquid assets Assets that are not easily converted into cash without the risk of serious loss, such as real estate, a business interest or art objects.

nonmarital (nonmarital deduction) trust A trust consisting of property that does not qualify for the marital deduction.

nonprobate property Property passing outside the administration of the estate. It passes other than by will or intestacy laws. Examples include jointly held property passing by right of survivorship (law), life insurance proceeds payable to a named beneficiary (by contract) and property in a living trust (property not titled to an individual).

nonresident alien Usually the noncitizen (alien) spouse of a deceased U.S. citizen. Special rules apply to prevent this spouse from removing property from the United States. Use of the marital deduction is usually not allowed unless certain conditions are met.

nonskip The transfer of property to the next-in-line generation. A father transfers property directly to his children as opposed to his grandchildren.

nuncupative will An oral will dictated by the testator before witnesses during a final illness and later converted to writing.

objectives In estate planning, the formulation of each individual's needs and desires regarding distribution of his or her estate and the various intricacies involved in the transfer.

1 percent solution A formula involving 1 percent of the total gross estate to fund the purchase of life insurance inside an irrevocable trust. The purpose is to provide liquidity for estate tax payment or to replace the loss of estate property due to taxation on a leveraged basis.

operation of law Assets that pass outside of a probate estate by certain ownership. Property held between spouses as joint tenants with rights of survivorship passes to the surviving tenant by operation of law.

optimal marital deduction Using the unlimited marital deduction in a trust arrangement to gain a tax liability of $0 at the death of the first spouse.

outright ownership Assets that pass directly to another individual at death. Complete ownership of property by an individual.

payable on death (POD) An arrangement whereby a depositor elects that a sum of money or account be payable to named individuals upon death. Similar to a beneficiary arrangement.

per capita A way of distributing an estate so that the surviving descendents will share equally, regardless of generation.

personal representative A person appointed by the court to settle an estate.

per stirpes A way of distributing an estate so that the surviving descendents will receive only what their immediate ancestor would have received if he/she had been alive at the time of death.

posthumous child A child born after its parents' deaths.

pourover Refers to the transfer of property from one estate or trust to another estate or trust, triggered by the occurrence of an event such as a death. For example, property disposed of by will can "pour over" into an existing trust.

power of appointment The right given to a donee to dispose of property that he or she does not fully own, within the limits set forth by the donor. This can cause the value of the asset to be included in the estate of the person who holds the power of appointment.

present interest As applied to a gift, the present right to use or enjoy the property. A gift must have this characteristic to qualify for the annual $10,000 gift tax exclusion.

pretermitted heir A child or other descendant omitted from a testator's will.

principal The property funding a trust, from which income is expected to be earned. Trust principal is also known as *res* or *corpus*.

probate The process of providing the validity of a will in court and executing its provisions under the guidance of the court. When a person dies, the will must be filed before the proper officers of the court, giving the court jurisdiction in the matter to enforce the document commonly referred to as "filing the will for probate." When the will has been filed, it is said to be "admitted to probate." The process of probating a will involves recognition by the court of the personal representative named in the will (or appointment of an administrator if none has been named), the filing of proper reports and papers as required by law, determination of validity of the will if it is contested and distribution and final settlement of the estate under the supervision of the court.

probate property Property that passes under the terms of a will. If there is no will, it passes under the state intestacy laws.

qualified charity A charity that qualifies to receive gifts for which an income tax charitable deduction is allowable.

qualified domestic trust (QDOT) A special trust to which assets are transferred so that a spouse who is not a U.S. citizen (a nonresident alien) will be entitled to claim the benefit of the unlimited marital deduction.

qualified terminable interest property (QTIP) Property qualifying for the marital deduction at the election of the donor or the decedent's personal representative. The spouse retains a qualified income interest in the property for life, with the income payable at least annually. The corpus ultimately passes to a specified remainderman, under a special power of appointment given to the spouse.

qualified terminable interest trust (QTIP trust) A trust that qualifies for the unlimited marital tax deduction. There will be no estate tax on the value of the property transferred to the surviving spouse in a QTIP trust on the first spouse's death as long as the surviving spouse receives all income at least annually. The purpose of the QTIP trust is to enable an estate to avoid tax, while the grantor still designates who will receive the property remaining in the trust on the second spouse's death.

quarterback An estate planner who specializes in the practice of estate planning and who coordinates the entire effort for a client. This involves designing the plan, based on the objectives; suggesting a format; and executing the plan in conjunction with other professionals or providing outlets for the accounting, legal and all additional aspects of execution.

remainder interest A future interest that comes into existence after the termination of a prior interest. For example, individual A creates a testamentary trust under a will in which the principal is to be retained with income paid to individual B until B's death, at which time the principal or remainder interest will be passed to individual C.

remainderman The person who is entitled to receive the principal of a trust when the intervening life estate or estates terminate.

remedy of partition The separation of shares of property held jointly by the direction of a court.

residuary estate The remaining part of a decedent's estate after debts, expenses and distributions have been made. Wills usually contain a clause on disposing of the residue of the estate that the decedent has not otherwise bequeathed.

reverse QTIP The use of a QTIP trust to preserve a decedent's $1 million generation-skipping exemption.

reversionary interest The possibility that property will return to the donor after it has been given away.

reversionary trust A trust limited to a specified term of years or for the life of the beneficiary. At the end of that period, the trust is terminated and the property is returned to the grantor.

revocable living trust A written legal document into which you place all of your property, with instructions for its management and distribution upon your disability or death.

revocable trust A trust that can be altered, amended, terminated or revoked during the grantor's lifetime with all property being recovered by the grantor.

right of survivorship Property held jointly whereby at the death of one joint owner, the other owner or owners succeed to full ownership by surviving under law.

semiliquid assets Assets that can be converted to cash within a reasonable amount of time—usually within one year.

settlor Another term for the grantor or creator of a trust.

shrinkage A reduction in the amount of property that passes at death caused by loss of capital and income resulting from payment of death costs. It may be greatly increased if assets must be sold for cash to pay such costs.

skip person In generation-skipping transfers, the person of the generation that is skipped. The child of a parent who makes gifts favoring only grandchildren is considered a skip person.

sprinkling or spray trust A trust under which the trustee is given discretionary powers to distribute any of the income among beneficiaries in equal or unequal shares and to accumulate any income not distributed.

state death tax credit A format of many states to calculate and collect their portion of state-imposed death taxes.

step-up-in-basis A decedent's capital gains property that passes to others escaping capital gains tax when sold by the person who inherits the property. Persons inheriting capital gains property receive the property at date-of-death fair market value. In effect the basis in this property is deemed to be "stepped up" and does not reflect the decedent's original cost basis for determining applicable capital gains tax on the sale of the property.

super trust A package of trust instruments that includes a revocable living trust, an A/B bypass trust and an irrevocable life insurance trust.

tangible property Property that has physical substance, such as a house or car.

taxable distributions Distributions from qualified retirement plans that are fully taxable. These can also refer to distributions from a trust when working with generation-skipping transfers.

taxable terminations In generation-skipping transfers, interests in trusts that terminate (e.g., income rights).

Tax Reform Act of 1986 (TRA '86) A wide-encompassing tax act that made many changes in estate and gifting rules.

tenancy by entirety Ownership of property by a husband and wife so that such property may not be disposed of during life by either spouse without the other's consent. Upon death, the property goes to the survivor.

tenancy in common Ownership of property by two or more persons so that each has an undivided interest that at the death of one, is passed by will to the deceased's heirs. It does not pass automatically to the surviving tenants in common.

terminable interest An interest in property that will terminate in the future. Usually associated with the right to income from a trust that terminates at the death of the grantor.

testamentary The passing of property at death by will.

testamentary trust A trust set up in a will that only takes effect after death.

testate A person who dies with a will.

testator, testatrix A person who dies with a will. A male is a *testator;* a female is a *testatrix.*

transferee The person receiving property transfers.

transferor The person who makes transfers of property to others.

trust An arrangement for holding legal property and managing the property for the benefit of another.

trustee The holder of legal title to property for the management, use or benefit of another.

unfunded insurance trust An insurance trust that is not provided with cash or securities to pay the life insurance premium. Such premiums usually are paid by someone other than the trustee.

unified credit An amount up to $600,000 in assets that every taxpayer is allowed to exclude from the estate and gift tax.

unified credit against estate tax A credit of up to $192,800 in 1987 and later years that can be applied directly against the federal estate tax to the extent that it has not been applied to gift tax obligations.

unified credit against gift tax A credit of up to $192,800 in 1987 and later years that can be applied directly against the federal gift tax but thereby reduces the available unified credit against estate tax.

unified credit trust In spousal estates, a trust designed to hold part of or the full unified credit amount ($600,000) at the death of the first spouse. (See **family trust**.)

unified probate code A standardized probate process adopted by many states in an effort to simplify the probate process.

unitrust (See **charitable remainder trust**.)

unlimited marital deduction Property that qualifies as marital deduction property. Under ERTA 1981, the ability to pass unlimited amounts of property that qualifies for the marital deduction became law. At present unlimited amounts of marital deduction property may pass to a surviving spouse without estate or gift tax consequences.

wealth replacement trust (WRT) An irrevocable life insurance trust that replaces the value of gifted assets made to charities used in conjunction with charitable remainder trusts (CRTs).

wealth transfer Process and strategies for transferring property to others with minimal estate and gift tax liability.

will A written document with instructions for disposition of property at death; can only be enforced through the probate court.

Index

THE NEXT STEP

☐ Please provide me with additional reports on the following:

☐ I need illustrations and numbers specific to my personal estate on the following:

☐ **Estate Planning Strategies for the 90s**   ☐ **Estate Analysis**

☐ **Revocable Living Trusts**   ☐ **Charitable Remainder Trusts**

☐ **Gifting**   ☐ **QTIP Trust Planning**

☐ **The 1 Percent Solution**   ☐ **Irrevocable Trusts**

☐ **Asset Protection**   ☐ **Estate Freeze Techniques**

☐ **Family Limited Partnerships**   ☐ **Corporations**

☐ **Tax on my IRA or retirement benefits**

YOUR FULL NAME			SPOUSE'S FULL NAME (if applicable)		
DATE OF BIRTH	CITIZENSHIP	OCCUPATION	DATE OF BIRTH	CITIZENSHIP	OCCUPATION

HOME ADDRESS	CITY, STATE, ZIP	HOME PHONE ( )
MAILING ADDRESS	CITY, STATE, ZIP	WORK PHONE ( )

☐ **I Request a Telephone Conference with an Estate Planner**

☐ **OTHER:**

RETURN TO:

BDC, INC.
1120 LINCOLN STREET, SUITE 708
DENVER, CO 80203

OR CALL THE AUTHORS AT

1-800-598-9406
1-800-223-9610